CORE BUSINESS PROGRAM

BUSINESS DATA PROCESSING

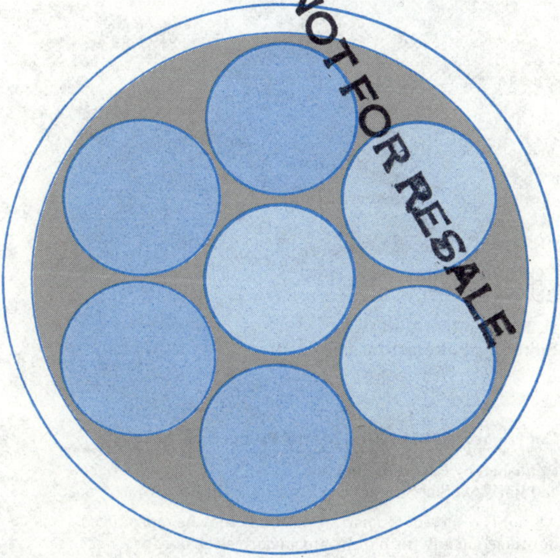

By
D. Hawgood

Edited by
F. Robert Jacobs

Facts On File Publications
460 Park Avenue South
New York, N.Y. 10016

CORE BUSINESS PROGRAM
BUSINESS DATA PROCESSING

D. Hawgood, MA, M.Inst.P, MBCS
Edited by: F. Robert Jacobs, Ph.D.

Published by Facts On File, Inc.
460 Park Avenue South, New York, N.Y. 10016

First edition published in the United Kingdom in 1983 by Mitchell Beazley London Ltd., Mill House, 87-89 Shaftesbury Avenue, London W1V 7AD, England.

Library of Congress Cataloging in Publication Data

Jacobs, Robert.
Business data processing.

1. Business—Data processing. I. Title.
HF5548.2.J234 1985 658'.054 84-8082
ISBN 0-8160-0051-4

Printed and Bound in Great Britain
1 0 9 8 7 6 5 4 3 2 1

Contents

Introduction

The transactions of business and the control of processes are accompanied by the storage and processing of information. The progress of technology has led to the development of a variety of aids to these activities. In particular, devices such as typewriters, calculators, mechanical accounting machines, and digital computers have been developed.

The electronic digital computer, for example, has decreased in cost and increased in speed to the extent that it has now taken its place in a great variety of different types of information processing. From being available to a limited number of people engaged in scientific and commercial data processing, computing has become a part of many professions. Today the digital computer has even become common in the home, where its tremendous educational and entertainment value are only beginning to be tapped.

The application of computers forces a logical analysis of the flow of information and the criteria for making decisions. These requirements have led to the development of a systems approach to analysis and use of information. Much of the success in the use of digital computer technology is dependent upon proper analysis of these requirements.

Computing cannot be studied in isolation from other topiics in business studies, since it affects many facets of a company from both a decision-making and information processing standpoint. This book is intended as an aid for all those studying computing as part of the many business disciplines which it assists. In doing so, it provides a compact statement of the core of knowledge required in computing. The reader is referred to the Further Reading section on page 118 for a list of books providing more detailed information.

Computing, in particular, is bedevilled by a profusion of technical terms, often with no uniformity in their usage by the different suppliers of equipment and services. The glossary on page 119, and several books in the Further Reading list, aim to clarify the terminology.

Chapter 1

Basis of Computing

COMPUTERS AND INFORMATION

Computing, printing, photography and sound recording are all forms of automatic information processing. In all of these processes, the information, as perceived by man, is captured, processed, transmitted and stored. Finally, it is reproduced in a form which can easily be understood by man.

The computer is a machine which automatically processes input **data**, in accordance with a **program** of instructions stored within the computer, and then provides the results in a useful form. The computer can combine several pieces of information in a preset way and provide a result different from the input, whereas the other forms of information processing mentioned above are generally attempting to re-create the input information. A distinction needs to be made between meaning and physical representation: information is the *meaning* which a human understands, whereas data are the *physical representation* of that information in a manner formalized for transfer to another human or machine.

Information is formalized when it is spoken or written, using the agreed sounds, letters, words and symbols of the particular language in use. In writing, strings of letters represent words and strings of digits represent numbers.

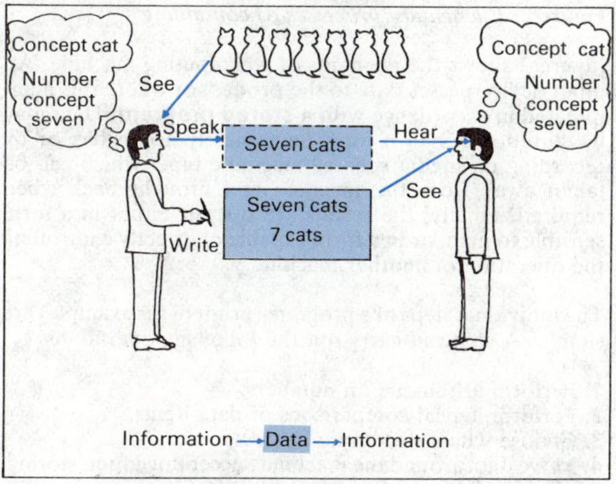

Figure 1. Information and data

Figure 1 shows the distinction between meaning and representation. One person asks ‘what can you see?’. The spoken or written reply by the other person is ‘seven cats’. In writing, we can spell out the number or represent it by the digit '7'. The syntax rules of the English language require that in this reply the number is placed first and the word cat is made plural by the addition of 's'. 'The seventh cat' would convey completely different information.

In information processing, the strings of data characters are manipulated while they are in the machine, without reference to their meaning. Data is sorted, selected and combined arithmetically or logically. To achieve this, the problem to be solved must first be analyzed and a detailed sequence of instructions prepared. This sequence of steps and decisions is called an **algorithm** for the solution of the problem; the equivalent sequence of instructions in a form which can be understood by the machine is a computer **program**.

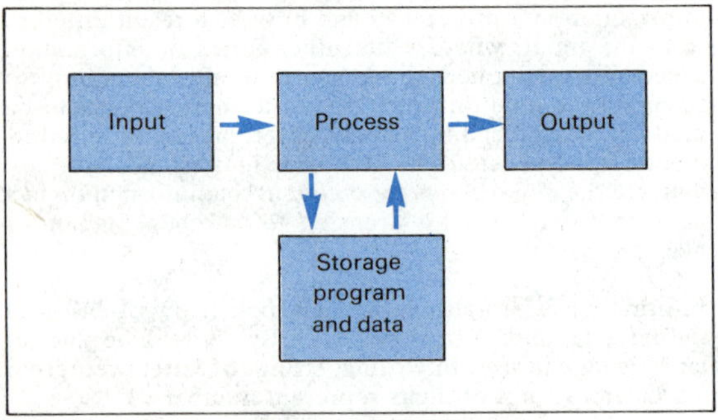

Figure 2. Elementary processes of computing

Figure 2 shows the elements of a computing machine. An input device passes data to the **processor** where it is manipulated in accordance with a **stored program**. Data may be stored either in a form immediately accessible, or by recording on media such as magnetic tape, which can be taken away from the machine and brought back when required. Finally, the results are **output** either in a form sensible to man, or in a form capable of directly controlling the operation of another machine.

The individual steps of a program (printed, for example) are simple. A step can carry out the following operations.

1. Perform arithmetic on numbers.
2. Perform logical comparisons of data items.
3. Choose which step to do next.
4. Move data around the machine–accepting input, storing, retrieving and providing output.

The following factors allow such simple steps to be built into the complex and sometimes confusing field of computing.

1. Speed Electronic computers perform thousands or even

millions of instructions per second, with input and output up to thousands of characters per second.

2. Accuracy and repeatability Once the program has been written it is followed in the same way time after time.

3. High volume A computer may have access to any one of millions of items of data within a millionth of a second, and access to thousands of millions of items of data within a second.

4. Complexity The simple program steps can be built up logically into procedures which may be difficult for a human to implement manually.

5. Cost Mass production and economy of scale reduce the cost of information processing, since the same process may be repeated for many items of data, and the same types of equipment can perform many different processing tasks.

6. Environment Although some large computers require a clean air-conditioned environment, others are built to function in conditions inhospitable to man, e.g. space, missiles.

7. Commonality Complex procedures are common to many organizations, e.g. tax for payroll, so the same set of simple steps can be used in many instances.

Types of computer
Computers may be subdivided into the following categories.

1. Digital computers operate on numbers as strings of discrete digits.

2. Analog computers operate on numbers as physical magnitudes, e.g., of voltage or angular position.

3. Hybrid computers are digital computers incorporating analog processing elements.

This book is concerned with digital electronic computers. These can be further subdivided into special-purpose or general-purpose computers.

1. Special-purpose machines are tailored and connected for one application only, e.g., traffic control, automobile ignition systems, arcade 'space invader' machines, etc.

2. General-purpose machines can be used for a number of different applications including business, scientific, educational, leisure and a whole multiplicity of information processing requirements.

Special-purpose computers perform their specific jobs as need arises, but general-purpose machines can do many different kinds of jobs.

1. Transaction processing This involves the query and updating of data managed by the computer. The term is particularly used where a number of terminals have access to the same program and stored data, e.g., in airline reservation systems. If the result is given immediately the computer is said to work in **real time.**

2. Batch processing Inputs are gathered together from various sources within an organization. The same process is performed on all inputs as a batch, often during a time period when computer usage would otherwise be low. The results are distributed, e.g. payroll.

3. Multi-access Many users at terminals are able to develop and run their own programs with their own stored data. The programs run independently, but are all stored in one computer.

Communications

Communications links may be used to connect computers with users. This allows the results of processing obtained from one computer to be used as input for another computer situated elsewhere, and provides remote input and output of data to terminals controlled by users. The major communications lines currently in use are those of the telephone system. Organizations based at a single site can use local cabling. These local systems of computers are often formed into local area networks which allows users to share the resources of many computers.

HISTORY OF COMPUTERS

Computers have developed as a result of the needs of the people to process information. As people required more speed in information processing and greater data storage capacity, computer technology flourished. Development of computer technology has caused significant changes in the way society operates.

Incorporation of the technology into a business may change the mix of skills required in the organization, and may result in many people losing their jobs, thus creating negative feelings toward its further development.

Computing has features which tend to isolate it in social terms. Information processing by computer is organized and formalized in a manner which many people dislike and find alien. Jobs change in a way which alters not only the content of the job, but also the way in which people have to think. The computer and its attendants appear to have enormous power, which can be used constructively or destructively. However, understanding can dispel fear, and so it is necessary to consider the precursors of computers.

By 500 BC, a counting board with pebbles in grooves was in use in ancient Greece. A descendant of this board, the **abacus**–with beads on wires–was developed in China and Japan, and is still widely used in the Middle and Far East for commercial calculations. The abacus preceded the posi-

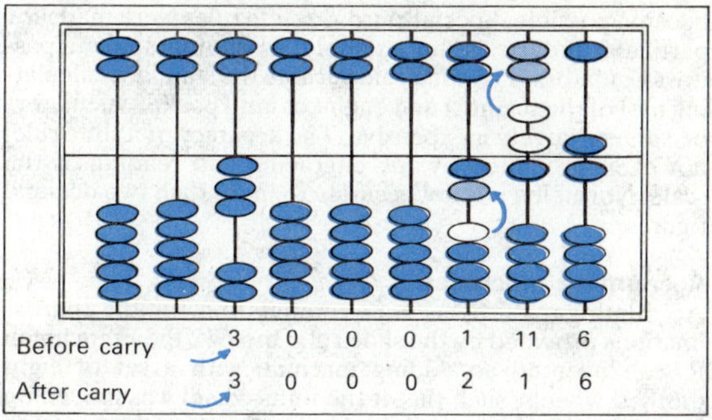

Figure 3. The abacus

tional numbering system and the invention of a symbol for zero. In the Chinese version, shown in Figure 3, there is a maximum of two beads above the bar and five beads below the bar on each wire. Each bead above the bar stands for five and each bead below the bar stands for one. The beads against the bar on a wire represent one decimal digit. Addition is performed by moving appropriate extra beads towards the bar, then making adjustments for any carry.

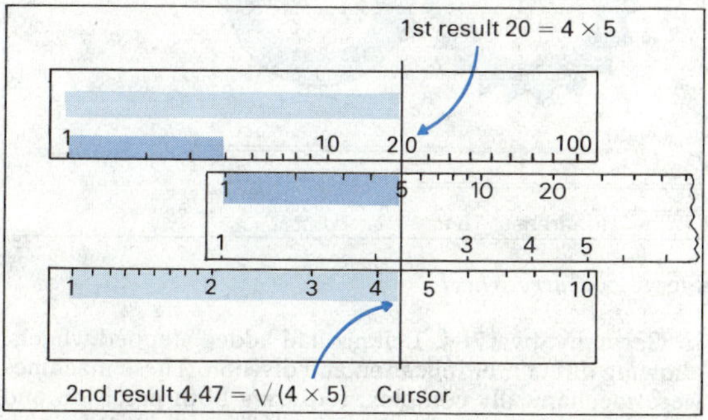

Figure 4. The slide rule

Napier (1550–1617) invented logarithms–numbers with the property that the sum of the logarithms of two numbers is the logarithm of their product. This allows multiplication and division to be performed by using addition and subtraction. By 1672 this principle had been applied to a calculating device–the **slide rule**. Ruled gradations are spaced logarithmically on two slides. Figure 4 shows the number 5 on the middle slide being multiplied by the number 4 on the top slide. There are two decades on the top slide and one on the bottom, arranged so that the number at any position on the top slide is the square of the number on the bottom slide, which allows the calculation of squares and square roots to be performed. With additional scales, and a fine line cursor across all scales, the calculation of trigonometrical functions became possible. Special-purpose slide rules were made for particular industries, for example, as photographic exposure calculators. The slide rule became the standard calculating tool of the scientist and engineer until pocket calculators became relatively inexpensive. The accuracy of a slide rule, however, is limited by the engraving and reading of the scale. Normally, it is not accurate to more than two decimal figures.

Accounting machines

Accounting requires accurate computation, not the approximations provided by the slide rule. In 1642 the Frenchman Pascal invented an adding machine with a set of eight toothed wheels, such that if the units wheel was moved on from '9' to '0' the carry was added to the tens wheel, and so on. A **'carry wheel'** mechanism is shown in Figure 5. Each decimal position has two wheels on a spindle, one with 20 teeth and one with 2 teeth. This allows the carry up or down, for addition or subtraction.

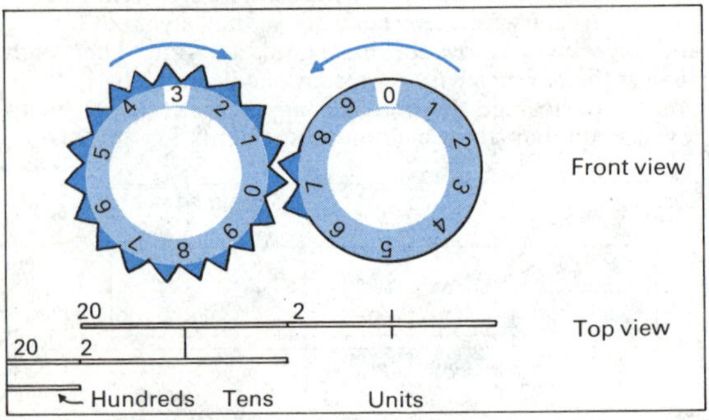

Figure 5. Carry wheel

In Germany, by 1704, Leibniz had added stepped wheels, allowing direct multiplication and division. These machines were mechanically complex, requiring both precision and strength. Initially, the machines built by Pascal and Leibniz were fragile and could not be made in quantity by the processes available at the time. However, technology soon caught up with the inventions, and accounting machines became the standard tool of European commerce.

These machines progressed in complexity and variety. Additional wheels or keyboards were introduced for initial setting of numbers. Other developments included wheels to accumulate running totals, printing on paper rolls or **ledger cards**. A typewriter keyboard allowed the customer's statement to be prepared and the supplier's sales ledger to be updated. The operation in this type of application was controlled by a **program bar**–a piece of metal with notches to control the sequence of operations and print positions of the mechanism. At the beginning of the transaction the operator keyed in the previous balance and account number. On some machines, methods of detecting errors in re-keying balances were incorporated, for example by adding the customer account number and balance. This **hash total** was recalculated at the beginning of a transaction and compared with the carried forward hash total.

Electronic accounting and visible record machines

As mechanical accounting machines developed, motors and relays were added and mechanical counting wheels were replaced by purpose-built electronic logic. **Magnetic ledger cards** also became available. The account number and old balance were recorded on a magnetic strip that ran down the card and were read into the machine as the card was inserted. These machines evolved into sophisticated accounting systems which could run at the local level of the organization and allow immediate management control. Their development continued in parallel with the growth of computing; as a by-product of ledger accounting, some machines punched **paper tape** which could be processed by computer for the provision of centralized management accounting. Electronic accounting machines are now merging into computing, with fixed logic being replaced by a **microcomputer** and ledger cards being replaced by **cassette tape** or **floppy disk**.

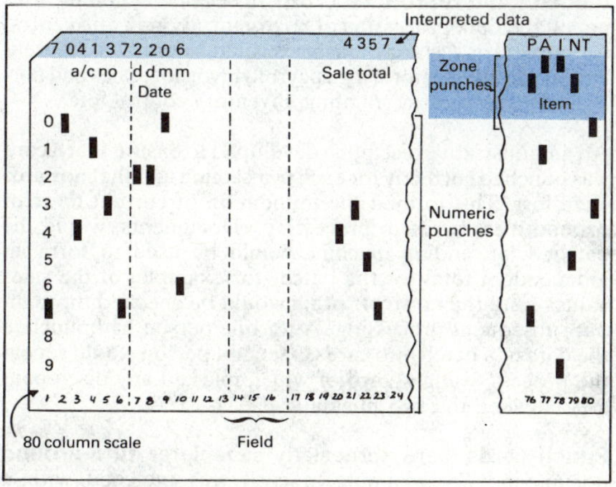

Figure 6. Punched card

Punched card systems

The weaving of complicated colored patterns requires the selection, in a predetermined order, of threads on a loom. In France, in the 18th century, Jacquard developed a loom in which the threads were selected by rods pressing through holes punched in cards. The pack of cards for a pattern could be stored for reuse. This system was itself a commercially successful method of machine control and in turn led to a method for the processing of high volumes of data.

It took over seven years to produce the first report on the 50 million inhabitants of the United States. Following the population census of 1880, the imminent 1890 census posed an interesting 'data processing' problem. A solution to the problem was developed by Hollerith in the form of an electromechanical machine which counted and tabulated cards encoded with data. For the 1890 census, the number and characteristics of people were encoded using a series of holes on cards. These are often referred to as punched cards.

Initially, the coding of information from a document to a punched card had become a separate operation from the tabulation of that information. Hollerith subsequently developed many machines for use in business. For example, the following type of activity could be performed. The **unit record** data of one business transaction was punched into one card. Cards could be sorted mechanically, placing all purchases by one customer together and collating them with cards containing name, address and previous balance. A **tabulator** printed a statement for the customer and punched a card with the new balance, ready for the next month's run.

Punched card processing required the use of a number of different machines working in sequence to **sort**, **collate**, **tabulate** and **reproduce** cards. It became economical to put all the data processing of an organization in one central department as the same machines could be used for different large-scale applications, e.g., payroll, invoicing, sales and purchase ledgers, cost accounting, inventory control, etc.

An administrative discipline developed to ensure that a card was punched correctly for each transaction and that no cards were lost. This formed the foundation of current **control procedures** in data processing. Documents would be batched, an adding machine would be used to form an independent total for the batch–for example, of the sales values–and the **control totals** would be checked throughout subsequent processing. After one person had punched the data of a batch into cards, a second person would repeat the process, using a **verifier** which marked any discrepancies between the two punchings.

Punch cards were particularly suitable as **turn-around** documents. For example, a card was punched with a magazine subscriber's account number and renewal date and, as the renewal date approached, sent to the customer, requesting a renewal. On receipt of the subscription the card was replaced in the addressing system to validate the subscription for another year. The convenience of physical sorting also led to the introduction of **aperture cards**, which could hold microfilm of engineering drawings and enabled cards to be sorted and selected as required.

Computing engines and computers

The origins of the computers themselves will now be considered. Babbage (1792-1871) was an English mathematician who realized that existing tables of logarithms and polynomials were inaccurate and so invented a **difference engine** to mechanize their production. His invention, which like Pascal's was in advance of the technology to produce it, belongs to the era of accounting machines. Babbage, however, went on to invent an **analytical engine** although he did not build one. If this machine had been built it would have been a **programmable digital mechanical computer**. It would have included the ability for one operation to change instructions held in the machine, and would have enabled branching to different sets of instructions depending on the result of a comparison.

A machine with these abilities was not built until 1944, when the electromechanical Automatic Sequence Controlled Computer (**ASCC**) was completed by Harvard University and IBM. In 1946, the Electronic Numerical Integrator And Calculator (**ENIAC**), which used 18 000 electronic valves, was completed at the University of Pennsylvania.

These machines used decimal digits for storage and calculation. Programs were set by the manual manipulation of hundreds of plugs, sockets and switches. In 1946, after a theoretical study of computing, Von Neumann proposed two fundamental changes. One of these was the use of **binary** instead of decimal arithmetic, as combinations of two-state electronic valves were being used inefficiently to hold decimal digits. The other change enabled **defined instructions** to be wired into the machine, each instruction being numbered with an **operation code**. The sequence of instructions was determined by the operation code number, held in the memory together with the memory locations of the numbers to be operated on, also held in memory.

Machines, in accordance with these principles, were then built at universities and research laboratories in the United States and Europe. Eventually, the valves used in these early computers were replaced by transistors and then later on by multi-element integrated circuits. Storage technology progressed: the **core store**, in which every stored bit is a ring of magnetic material threaded by three wires, was used for many years. Now, most immediate access memory is in the form of **semiconductor integrated circuits**.

Developments to produce faster and cheaper logic and storage elements have been accompanied by changes in the design of the structure of computers and of computer programs. Early machines obeyed one stored program written by a programmer in **machine code**, binary numbers representing addresses and operation codes. Later, computer **languages** were developed. The early languages were **assemblers**, which made the writing of machine code easier by the use of named labels for data items and addresses. They also supplied commonly used routines to be linked into user programs.

These assembler languages were written in terms of the machine's instruction set and were different for each manufacturer. In the late 1950s, **high-level languages** were developed that were independent of the features of the machine and used terms appropriate to the problem rather than the instruction set. COBOL, FORTRAN and BASIC were the first high-level languages to be used.

1. COBOL This is designed for business use and was developed for the US Department of Defense.
2. FORTRAN This is used for scientific work and was developed by IBM.
3. BASIC, an easy-to-learn language, developed at Dartmouth College.

In the 1960s, the development of computer systems was made easier by the introduction of software application packages. The further development of machines was facilitated by a **standard interface** approach, in which all peripherals for one manufacturer's range of equipment had one common method of connection to the processor. On powerful processors, **multiprogramming** and **timesharing operating systems** were developed to allow efficient use of the equipment and easier access for users. In the 1970s, the range of computers available became wider, with multiprocessor configurations and **virtual storage** techniques making the large machines more versatile. Today

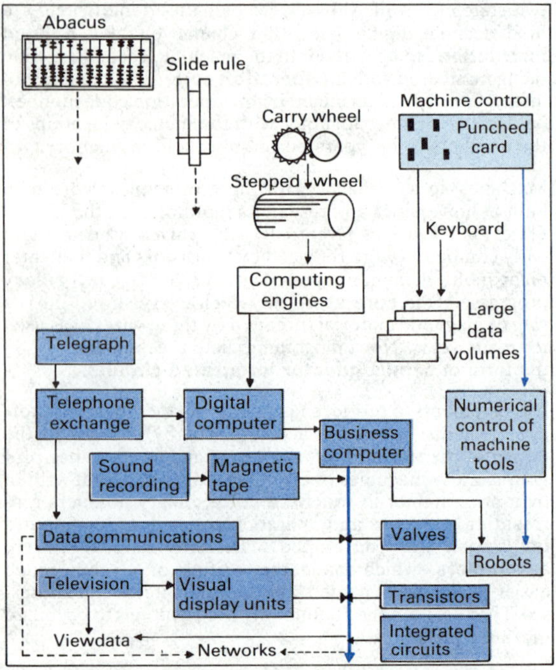

Figure 7. History of computing

inexpensive microprocessor-based 'personal computers' are enabling many more users to own or rent their own computer. Possible future developments in computing are discussed at the end of Chapter 10.

Communications

Although punched card systems were centralized, the movement of data to and from the data processing center was by physical transport of documents and cards. **Telex** and **teletype** systems, with keyboards, printers and paper tape readers and punches linked by telegraph wires, were developed in response to the need of railways to pass on information for signalling in advance of trains arriving.

Early computer communication used paper tape as the main transfer medium. This was due to the relative high speed of the paper tape reader. There have been great advances in communications technology since these early days. With the development of **multiprogramming**, it became feasible to assign one program to communications, with one or more remote teletypewriters connected **on-line** direct to the computer. Faster lines and cheaper **terminals** brought about a great expansion in the use of communications in computing. Today transmission rates of up to several thousand characters per second can be obtained over common telephone lines.

Machine control

In manufacturing, digital technology has been used as control mechanisms in machines. Initially, these were designed to make the machine repeat an exact cycle of operations consisting of specific cam settings, sequencers and linkages. These depended on a man minding the machine to adjust settings, feed material and watch for mishaps. Handling systems were added to give a constant supply of material; interlocks were introduced to stop the machine if the supply failed and instruments were included to set an alarm if the product was out of tolerance. As with the Jacquard loom, the cycle could be set by encoding information in punched holes; the use of **punched paper tape** increased with the development of **numerically controlled machine tools**.

In large plants, where the material output from one machine was the input to a further process, measurements and control circuits were wired to a central control room. If rules could be developed for this type of interaction, control could be performed by a **digital** or **analog process control computer** which, as a byproduct of control, could pass information on production to a business computer.

Development of microprocessors and the incorporation of these into manufacturing equipment allows both local and remote programmable control of machines. Today automated manufacturing systems are being developed by many companies which are flexible in their ability to be adapted to changing marketing and engineering requirements.

INFORMATION AND BUSINESS SYSTEMS

The study of business and public affairs can be split into a number of individual disciplines, which interact and overlap. The administration, control and decision-making of any organization depend on the flow of information.

Historically, information systems have adapted themselves to the available technology by using a variety of the following methods.

1. Messengers repeating verbal statements.
2. Coded representations–knots in string, smoke signals.
3. Writing.
4. Printing.
5. Electric wire systems–telegraph and telephone.
6. Electromagnetic radiation–microwave, radio, television, satellite.

For many centuries the formalities of business communication involved the writing, transmission and storage of messages on pieces of paper. Manual processsing of information generated further pieces of paper. The accounting discipline developed a set of standards for the ways in which information about money should be recorded. The discipline of organization and methods, associated particularly with the time and motion study of production methods, was also used in establishing efficient systems for the handling of the increasing volumes of paper involved in complex business organizations.

The movement, processing and storage of information have always been interconnected. These operations are all now changing from using paper to using systems involving electronic and magnetic technologies. Current information technology, in particular, relies heavily on disciplines of computing and telecommunications.

The change from paper systems necessitates the formalization and coding of information which requires precise definitions and careful attention to error detection. It has also led to changes in the nature of the organization itself–the economy of scale of large data-processing installations has led to greater centralization. But in many cases the information-processing to be performed is just the same as before. The basic commercial cycle of order, ship, invoice and payment, or a taxation cycle of identification, assessment and collection remains unchanged.

Information and its flow have to be formalized in the computer and so the development of a computer system necessitates the study of the nature of the information and the nature of the organization. This has encouraged a systems approach to the study of business and to the solution of problems, discussed further in Chapter 4.

The technology of information-processing is increasingly aligned to that of computing and, since information-flow is central to many disciplines of business, a knowledge of computing is becoming essential to those disciplines. Figure 8 shows the relationship between information, computing and business disciplines in an organization.

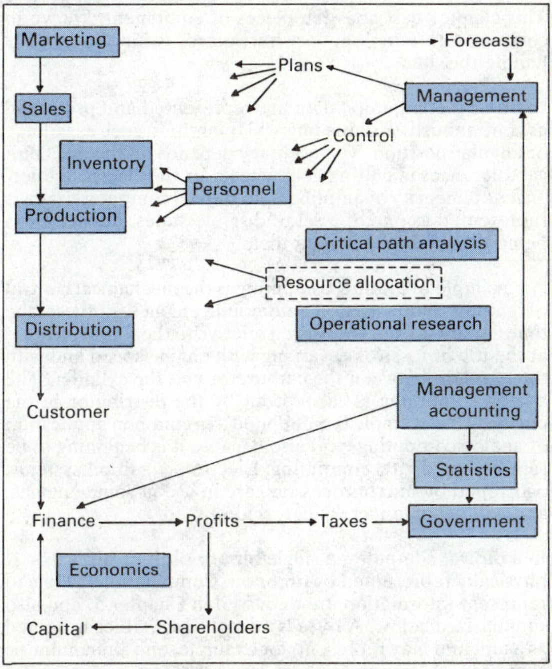

Figure 8. Information and business disciplines

Chapter 2

Computer Equipment

DIGITAL AND ANALOG COMPUTING

This chapter describes the pieces of equipment, known in computer terminology as **hardware**, which physically handle the data.

In **analog** computers, data are represented and processed as continuously variable physical quantities, such as voltage or angular position. The accuracy depends on the mechanical tolerances in cutting gear wheels, or the electrical tolerances of linearity of amplifiers. In **digital** computers, data is represented as one of a set of discrete states, the precision being the interval between them.

An example of **analog** computing is the mechanical control of ignition timing used in automobile engines. In these, the time a spark is fired is adjusted relative to the time a piston is at the top of its stroke, varying with engine speed and with the pressure between the carburetor and the cylinder. The analog computing is carried out by the distributor in the engine. This example is mentioned as a common application of analog computing, and also because it is beginning to be replaced by digital computing. Electronic ignition systems, controlled by microprocessors, are in use in some engines, and will become increasingly widespread.

In a **digital** computer, a single **binary digit** or **bit** is 0 or 1, physically represented by off or on. Combinations of bits to represent information are discussed in Chapter 5, and also summarized below. A **byte** is a set of 8 bits, which is treated as a unit and may represent, for example, one alphanumeric character. A combination of bytes to form a meaningful **data item** such as an account number or name is termed a **field**. A collection of fields relating to one occurrence of a set of variables is termed a **record**: an example would be the name, address, account number, outstanding balance and date of last transaction for a customer. The collection of records for a set of occurences, all customers, for example, is termed a **file**.

STRUCTURE OF A DIGITAL COMPUTER

A computer is a machine which accepts data, processes it and supplies results, under the control of a **stored program**. It has a **central processor** for computation and control, and a set of **peripherals** for input, output and storage. In considering the structure of a computer it is necessary to distinguish between flow of **data** and the passing of **control signals**. The **central processor** consists of:

1. **Control unit**.
2. **Arithmetic and logic unit**.
3. **Memory**, to hold data and instructions.

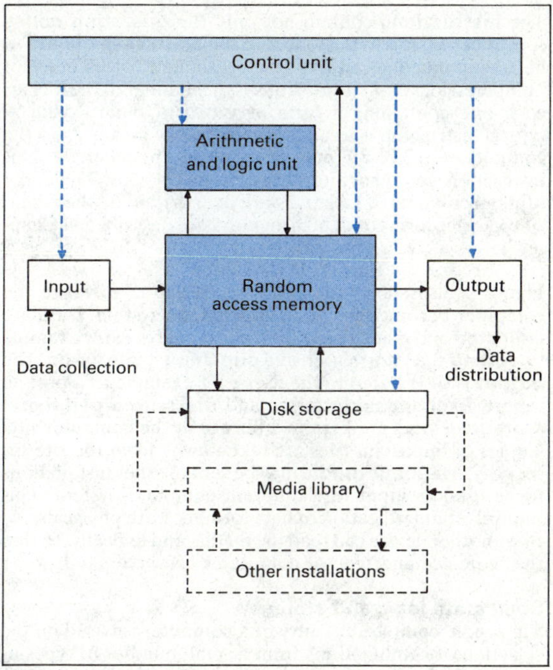

Figure 9. Structure of a digital computer

The sequence of events in operation is as follows.

1. The next **instruction** is **fetched** from memory to the control unit.

2. The control unit **decodes** the instruction, decides what events must follow from it, and sends **control signals** to appropriate units, as shown in Figure 9.

3. One of the following actions can now be initiated, all **data transfers** going to or from **memory**.

(a) **Fetch input** from peripheral.
(b) Wait for **interrupt** from specified input device.
(c) Send **output** from memory.
(d) **Read** data from **disk storage**.
(e) **Write** data to **disk storage**.
(f) Perform **arithmetic** on data items.
(g) Perform **logical operations** on data items.

4. By inspecting the results of an arithmetic or logic instruction, the control unit decides whether to proceed to the next in sequence or **jump** to a different instruction.

5. The cycle repeats, fetching the next instruction.

The **instructions** contain not only the **operation codes** specifying what is to be done, but the **addresses of data** to be manipulated. **Memory** can be thought of as a set of numbered lockers. The **address** is the number of the locker, each one containing a **byte** or **word** of binary data. A typical instruction is to add the contents of locker 75 to the contents of locker 29, putting the result in locker 29. This instruction would not alter the contents of locker 75, but the original contents of locker 29 are overwritten by the result. The various forms of data in memory are described in Chapter 4.

Figure 9 also shows the processes required to make the computer become part of an information system. **Data** are **collected** and made ready for the input device, for example by **coding** the information and **punching** it into **cards**. The **output** is distributed to the users, for example as a printed report. **Exchangeable tapes** and **disks** from **peripheral storage** devices are kept in a **library** at the computer site. Copies of important files are taken away from the site for security. **Magnetic media** may be sent to other installations to be used as input to a different computer system. This requires standardization of data formats, both physically, so that another device can read the media, and logically, so that the sequence and type of data items can be agreed.

Solid state logic and storage

The whole complex circuitry of a computer is based on the selection of combinations from a small number of types of **electronic logic gate**, formed as switching elements in a **semiconducting integrated circuit**. An example is the **AND** gate, with one output signal which is on only when all input signals are on together. Other logic gates are discussed in Chapter 5.

A variety of magnetic and semiconducting devices have been used for computer memory. **Magnetic core** memory was the usual form for many years, so the main memory was habitually called core memory. **Magnetic bubble** memory is also used now, although not as much as anticipated. Core memory uses individual magnetic rings threaded by wires whereas the construction of bubble memory is similar to that of integrated circuits: a sheet of magnetic material has patterns of conductors imposed on it. Signals in these create, shift and sense magnetized areas or bubbles. The majority of computers, however, now use integrated circuits of semiconducting devices for random access memory.

Whereas **Random Access Memory (RAM)** allows immediate access where contents can be retrieved and changed in the computer, data in **Read Only Memory (ROM)** cannot be changed in the computer; it is written on special devices using higher voltages. Its use enables a program to be kept available without the need to load it from disk storage and without the risk of it being corrupted accidentally. It is commonly used in microprocessors.

A byte of data can be moved around the computer either simultaneously as a pulse on 8 wires in **parallel**, or on one wire, as a train of 8 pulses **serially**, which is a cheaper method but slower.

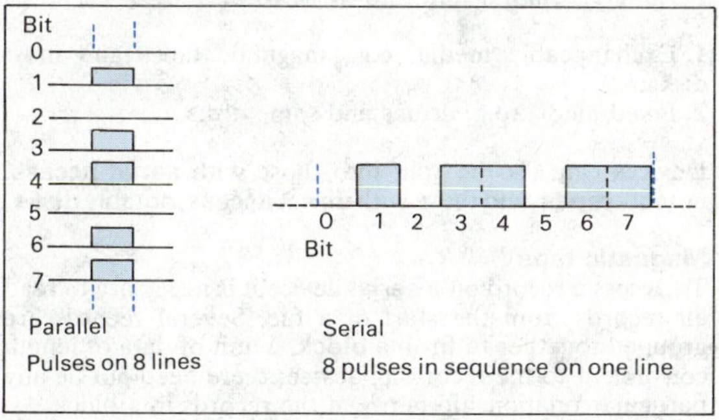

Figure 10. Serial and parallel data transfer

Each device attached to the processor may have its own **port** or **channel**. Alternatively one set of connectors may be taken as a **highway** or **bus** linking all the channels, a particular device accepting data only when its own address is set.

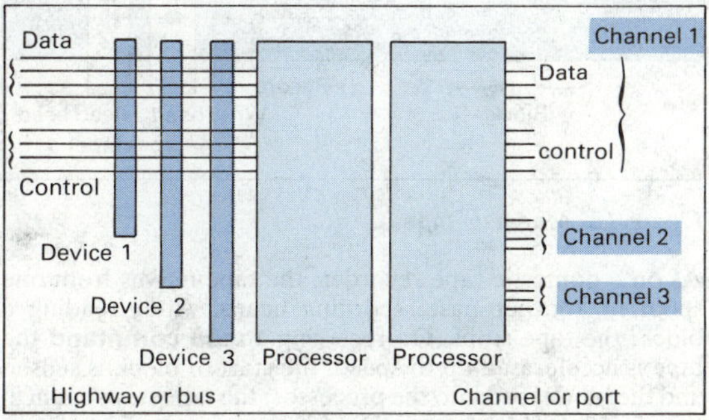

Figure 11. Interfaces as channels or highways

The two methods are likely to be combined in one computer, with separate channels for fast devices such as disks but a number of slow input/output peripherals on one bus.

In the performance of a computer system the **throughout capacity** of the channels and the way they are allocated to different **peripherals** can be more important that the number of instructions executed per second.

PERIPHERAL STORAGE DEVICES

A peripheral storage is one on which large amounts of data

can be stored and later retrieved and updated. Peripheral storage devices currently in use are based mainly on magnetic recording.

Peripherals can be split into those with:

1. Exchangeable media, e.g., magnetic tapes and most disks;
2. Fixed media, e.g. drums and some disks.

Devices can also be split into those with **serial access**, notably **tapes**, and those with **direct access**, notably **disks**.

Magnetic tape

To access a record on a **serial** device it is necessary to read all records from the start of a file. Several records are grouped together to form a **block**, a unit of data of length convenient to the recording device; there need not be any particular relationship between the records in a block.

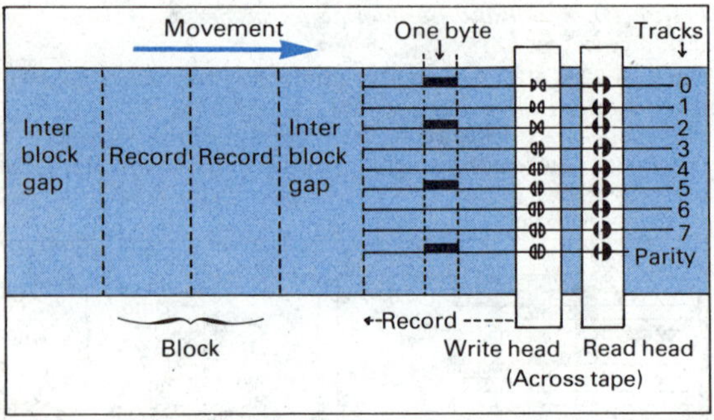

Figure 12. Magnetic tape

As on a domestic tape recorder, the tape moves from one spool to another past recording heads. After reading a block, the tape stops. On receiving a **read command** the tape is accelerated up to speed, the start of block is sensed and the block read into the processor; the tape stops again in the next **interblock gap**. Data in certain special records, e.g. **end of file**, can be recognized by the tape unit, allowing an instruction like 'skip to next file'. Unless interblock gaps are very long it is not possible to read a block, move back and write an amended version in the same place. The start and end of the tape have reflective markers detected by photocells.

There are various **formats**, the most common for large computer installations being **9-track tape**, on which nine heads record a track each, a byte being recorded on eight tracks across the tape; the ninth track contains **parity**–an additional bit generated from the other eight in such a way as to allow detection of errors in subsequent handling of the data. Parity is described further in Chapter 5. A read head after the write head allows an immediate check that data have been recorded correctly.

On **cassette tape**, often used with **microcomputers**, data are recorded serially on one track at a time.

Disks and direct access

In direct access devices any individual block of records can be accessed without reading all of the other records from the start of the file. A block can be changed and replaced in the same position without disturbing other blocks. A variety of physical devices have been used, including **magnetic cards**, **drums** and **loops of tape**, but **disks** are by far the most frequently used. The description that follows is of a multi-surface disk unit with one set of moving heads.

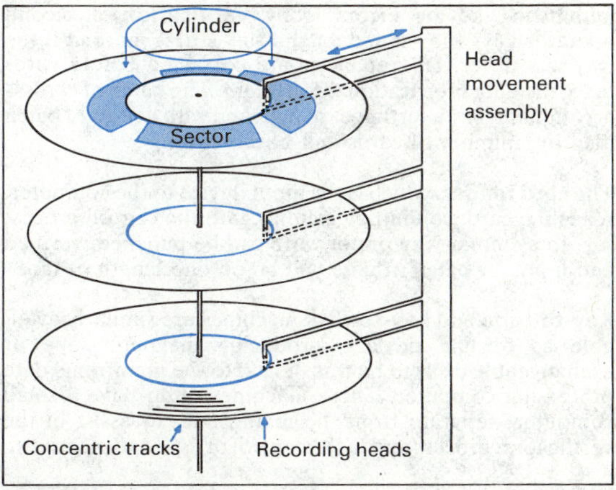

Figure 13. Multi-surface disk unit

The **disk pack** is an assembly containing up to eleven plates, whose surfaces are coated with magnetic material. It is loaded onto the **disk drive** in the same way as a record is loaded onto a record player. **Recording heads**, one per surface, move in and out, in unison, to any one of two hundred concentric circular **tracks**. Each track is divided into **sectors** which are the units of data that may be accessed, and which contain one or more **records**. The terms used for the subdivisions of data on disks vary greatly between manufacturers; disks with various numbers of surfaces, tracks and sectors are available.

Because the time taken to move the heads from track to track is much longer than the rotation time, it is convenient to consider the set of tracks at one head position as a **cylinder**. The address is given by the cylinder, surface and sector numbers. Every sector contains the same number of recorded characters, although those further out on the disk are physically longer.

A **floppy disk** unit is a similar device with magnetic coating on a single flexible plastic sheet; these units are cheaper but slower than the disk packs, and are used in many microcomputer systems. The multi-surface rigid disks have, by contrast, become known as **hard disks**.

INPUT DEVICES

In Figure 9 a distinction is made between the two separate phases of **data collection**, in which information is coded and prepared on machine readable media, and **input**, in which the data is read into the computer. Taking cards as an example, for **data preparation** a **card punch** is used which is an **off-line** piece of equipment, not connected to the computer. If a key is depressed, a coded pattern of holes, as shown in Figure 6, is punched into the card. One method of minimizing keying errors is by **verification**–a second operator keys the same data and the card is marked if the two sets differ. Discrepancies are corrected before cards leave the data preparation department. The batch of cards is accompanied by a further card punched with details of batch identity, number of cards and **batch total**.

The **card reader**, which is the input device to the computer, reads the card, column by column, into the central processor. In a similar way **paper tape** can be punched, verified and input. A batch of data will be on one length of tape.

Key-to-tape and **key-to-disk** machines are similarly available as off-line devices, producing magnetic tape or exchangeable disks to be transferred to the mainframe data processing computer. These machines often have a small computer, separate from the mainframe, to assist in the verification process and in the control of tape or disk drives.

Input devices, which sense marks or characters printed on paper by moving them past a reading head, are important because they minimize keying of data.

1. Magnetic Ink Character Recognition (MICR) is used in banking applications. Checks supplied to a customer have the account number and bank branch number printed in magnetic ink along the bottom in stylized characters. The amount is encoded in the same way at the branch where the check is paid in. All subsequent sorting and processing can be performed by machine. The MICR character set contains numbers and a few special characters only, and can be read by machine even when the document has been handled and soiled.

2. Optical Mark Recognition (OMR) The user marks lines with a pencil across selected boxes printed on a sheet of paper. The answering of multiple choice examination questions is one example of their use. Completed papers are collected into a batch and passed through a reader connected to the computer; papers with misplaced or incomplete lines are rejected by the machine into a separate pile.

3. Bar Code Readers Many products sold in supermarkets have a bar code printed on the packaging, encoding a number allocated by a standards committee to the manufacturer and a number allocated by the manufacturer to a particular product. By passing the bar code over a **laser beam** and **detector** at the supermarket checkout, the code number is input to the computer which then updates the inventory record for that product and sends the price to the cash register.

4. Optical Character Recognition (OCR) The readers recognize characters printed in particular typefaces. The most common form of these are readers which automatically feed and read printed documents. A familiar example is the reading of computer printed bills from public utilities and credit card companies, where a line at the bottom of the bill contains the customer number and amount. After encoding the actual amount paid, statements received back are batched and input, updating the customer's record on the sales ledger. This is an example of the **turn-around** document, widely used to minimize error and effort in the keying of data. Readers are also available to read a page which has been printed or typed in a standard typeface.

5. Recognition of hand-printed characters Machines are now available which can read handwritten characters. The characters must be the same as a model, within given levels of tolerances, so this method is mainly used where a group of staff is collecting data, e.g. electricity meter readings. Techniques in this field are progressing to allow the hand-printing of numbers by the general public as computer input.

6. Hand-held OCR wands passed over labels on products are used in production control systems and retail point of sale applications. A special typeface **OCR A**, stylized for ease of machine recognition, is often used with wand readers.

Input from analog devices

Many instruments can provide direct input to computers by the use of **analog–digital converters**. An example is a shaft position encoder, which would be used when replacing analog by digital control in an automobile engine. Some devices are specially designed for computer input, e.g., the joystick of a computer games machine, and plotters on which a pencil is moved over a tablet to input points from a graph or picture.

Input–output terminals

1. Keyboard printers (teletypewriters) are like electric typewriters with the addition of an interface to the computer. The input the user types and the reply from the computer are both printed.

2. Visual display units are similar to keyboard printers but they display the keyed characters and computer replies on a cathode ray tube. The display can be of characters, lines and areas of color. Special **graphics terminals** with fine resolution are used for engineering design and similar applications. A rapidly expanding field is the use of domestic television receivers with the addition of a keyboard and a telephone or cable link as a computer terminal.

OUTPUT

Magnetic tapes and **exchangeable disks** taken from one computer to another are, in effect, output from one and input to the other. For example, a firm's payroll system can output a magnetic tape, which is then input to the bank's computer as instructions to transfer money to the employees' accounts.

A **card punch** as an **on-line peripheral** is used to output data. This is now used mainly in turn-around systems. For example, a card punched with a product code and a process code may accompany a batch of parts; the return of the card to the computer shows that the process has been completed, and the production control system can schedule the next process. In some factory **shop-floor data collection** systems, **terminals** are used which incorporate **card-readers** for this purpose.

Paper tape punches have been used extensively for transferring data between computers, or from computers to numerically controlled machine tools. The use of paper tape is now largely being replaced by communications links or transfer of magnetic media.

Printing is such an important method of output that a wide variety of techniques are used, and changes to give cheaper or faster printers have developed rapidly. The most important techniques currently in use are given below.

1. There are several techniques in which the **shape of the letter** is pressed through the ribbon onto the paper.

(a) **Daisywheel printers** are used in **word processing**. The mechanism is moved to the column, rotated to the character, and fired. A typical speed is 80 characters per second. The print quality is excellent and the method is fairly cheap.
(b) A **barrel** printer has a rotating cylinder with a line of each character shape, and a hammer per print position. Hammers are fired as the correct character on the barrel comes round. All As in a line are printed, then all Bs, etc. A typical range is 300–1500 lines per minute, but the method is expensive.
(c) A **chain**, **train** or **band** of characters moves across the paper and a hammer per column fires at the appropriate time, e.g., if a line starts 'ABC' the first three hammers would fire at the same time. A typical range is 300–2500 lines per minute, but the method is expensive.

2. A **matrix printer** has a head with a matrix of fine wires which moves across the paper, and selected wires are moved forward to print a character shape. A typical range is 40–300 lines per minute and the method is cheap.

3. Laser printers use the principles of xerographic photocopiers. A moving light beam is modulated to form the character shapes, and then projected onto a photosensitive drum together with a letterhead or similar form outline. Ink sticks where the drum has been exposed, and is then pressed onto the paper. The range is 2000 to 15 000 lines per minute but the method is very expensive.

The characteristics determining the choice of printer are print quality, cost, speed, use of special paper, and ability to make several copies simultaneously. All the printers listed above use plain paper and all except the laser printer make multiple copies; the daisy wheel and laser printers give correspondence quality printing. For general use, most terminals and small computers use matrix printers, whereas large computer installations use barrel, chain, train or band printers.

The two types of device listed below print onto photographic film.

1. Computer Output to Microform (COM) devices print bulk computer output directly onto **microfilm** or **microfiche**. Multiple copies of the microform can then be made–an envelope can be mailed containing the equivalent of thousands of sheets of printed paper. Banks use this method for holding account details at branches, and booksellers can obtain on microfiche lists of all books in print.

2. Phototypesetters can project characters from a master copy of a typeface, enlarging and spacing characters as required, to form a photographic master for printing.

Sound output At its simplest, a musical note is generated by programming the delay between repetitions of a pulse sent to a loudspeaker. To achieve simulations of musical instruments or speech, it is necessary to encode the amplitude, the frequency distribution and the time decay of sounds. The output to the loudspeaker is then generated by a synthesizer incorporating digital/analog conversion. Speech may also be generated by a combination of elements from a recording of someone talking.

Machine control output can take a low-level binary signal and switch a solenoid, for example to open a cash drawer. Alternatively, **digital** signals can be converted to **analog** and applied to a motor, with **feedback input**. This type of control is used in **robots**, and as the number of robots increases it will become a more common form of output.

DATA TRANSMISSION

Data may be transmitted around the computer site using an

extension of the **bus** system (see Figure 11) or by using a **serial** interface (see Figure 10).

To extend this into the public telephone network, digital signals have to be converted to analog. This is done by a **modem** (**mod**ulator/**dem**odulator) at each end of the telephone line. This conversion is necessary because telephone lines were developed to carry human voice as analog data rather than digital data used by the computer.

Voice communication occupies a frequency band from about 300 to 3300 cycles per second. A high-quality telephone channel for voice can be used to transmit up to 9600 bits per second; the quality is affected by the bandwidth available and the noise and interruptions on the line. The telephone company or other telecommunications carrier uses **wideband** channels, often with **microwave** links, to group a number of voice circuits together.

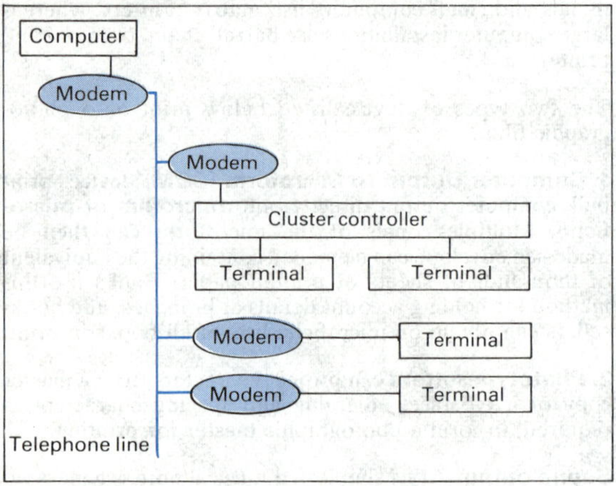

Figure 14. Multidropped Lines

In cases where terminals are used conversationally a line with a single terminal may be idle much of the time. To make better use of a private line leased from the carrier, it can be **multidropped** by connecting it from location to location. Each location has a **modem** with one or more **terminals**, each with its own address. To prevent all terminals trying to use the line together a **communications protocol** is established: some of those established by particular manufacturers or by international committees provide standards so that equipment from different manufacturers can be connected.

An extension of the multidropping concept is to a **packet switched network** or **ring**. A number of independent computers can be connected on one line. A message is injected into the network and passed along until it reaches the computer with the correct address.

Various levels of message checking can be incorporated.

1. A **parity** bit can be added to each character.
2. A **cyclic redundancy check** may be added to the message.
3. A **message sequence number** can be used.

The receiving end then checks these and, if there is a discrepancy, requests retransmission by sending back an agreed code message.

As the message is on public networks it is open to interception, so **encryption** may be used to protect data.

Chapter 3

Software

BASIS OF A COMPUTER PROGRAM

The central processor of a computer system consists of the control unit, the arithmetic and logic unit, and the memory. The memory contains a program of instructions specifying the sequence of operations needed to carry out a procedure, and also contains data to be manipulated by the operations.

The **software** of a computer system comprises all the programs which run on the computer for any purpose.

This chapter describes **machine** code, **assembler** and **high-level language** programming, and **system software**, which controls the operation of the machine. **Data base management systems** are described in Chapter 5 and **applications packages** in Chapter 9.

The basis common to all programs can be illustrated by considering the control of a machine for filling packets of screws (see Figure 15). This is a simplified example of the type of application for which microprocessors were

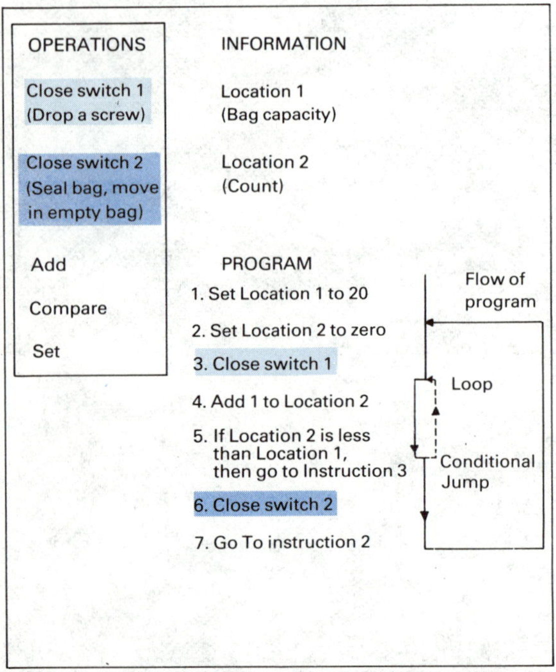

Figure 15. A simple packaging control program

developed, and as they get cheaper it becomes economic to use them for such simple applications rather than design a circuit for this purpose alone.

This simple example illustrates the distinctive features of a computer program.

1. Both program steps and data are held in a similar form in memory.
2. Information is referred to by the address at which it is stored in memory.
3. The steps of a program are stored in successive locations in memory.

The **control** unit holds the **address** of the next **instruction** in sequence. However, an instruction can cause a **jump** to an instruction in a different location. Thus, in our example in Figure 15, instruction 7 always causes a jump to instruction 2. Instruction 5 is a **conditional jump**–if the count is less than the capacity it transfers control to instruction 3; the sequence of instructions 3, 4, 5 is a **loop** which continues until the bag is full–then the **test** in instruction 5 fails, control passes on to instruction 6 instead of jumping, and the machine starts filling another bag.

MACHINE CODE AND ASSEMBLY LANGUAGE

A program in machine code is written in binary characters which, when placed in memory, can be directly obeyed by the processor. For example, in a typical microcomputer the machine code for the instruction 'compare the contents of the **accumulator** to the **operand** in address 8193' is the byte '10111110' followed by the two bytes representing 8193; '00100000' and '00000001'. The numbers have been written out to show in graphic terms why programmers avoid writing in binary!

In a program written in **assembly language**, each instruction written by the programmer corresponds to one machine code instruction, but it is written in **mnemonic** form and may allow the programmer to refer to a location in memory by a **symbolic name**.

For example, the comparison of the accumulator to a location accumulating a count could be 'CP COUNT'. To convert this assembly language to machine code, the **source code** mnemonics written by the programmer are entered into the computer as data, and processed by an assembler program to generate **object code** instructions with symbolic names converted to numeric memory locations. The assembly language may give additional facilities, for example the use of **macros** as a shorthand to incorporate frequently used series of instructions.

HIGH LEVEL LANGUAGES

Programs written in assembly language have three disadvantages.

1. There is a different language for each different type of computer.
2. Even a simple operation may need a large number of instructions.
3. The programmer has to think in terms of the computer, not in terms of the problem.

High level languages were introduced to provide a degree of compatibility between machines, and to allow the programmer to write instructions in a terminology appropriate to the problem.

COBOL is the most widely used business-oriented language. **FORTRAN** and **BASIC** are the most commonly used scientific/mathematical languages.

Each **statement** of any high level language has to be converted to a considerable number of machine code instructions, and variable names have to be allocated to storage locations in memory. This is generally done by a program called a **compiler**. The source code is compiled once only to give an object code which is output to an external storage device: to run the program the object code is loaded into the processor.

For **interactive** languages, for example **BASIC**, an alternative approach can be used. The source code is loaded into the processor each time the program is to be run, and when each statement comes to be obeyed it is passed through an **interpreter**. This turns it into machine code which is used immediately, then discarded. The use of an interpretive language eliminates the overhead of compilation runs, but it slows down the execution of the program when it is to be run.

Features of a program in a high level language

The BASIC program of Figure 16 illustrates a number of features common to most high level programming languages. The figure shows selected lines from a program for computer-aided learning, with a number of questions requiring yes/no answers. The path through the program depends on the answers keyed by the user in reply to questions displayed on the screen.

Assignment, **input/output**, **program development aids**, **comment**, **sub-routines** and **error routines** are all illustrated here in **BASIC**. The structure of statements for these may be different in other languages, to suit the type of problem, but the principles are the same.

At line 200, the **variable** *Q10$* is assigned the value *'QUESTION 10. IS AN ASSEMBLER A HIGH LEVEL LANGUAGE?'* The type of variable (**string** of characters, integer, single precision number, etc.) is declared – in this case giving the variable name *Q10$*. The final character $ declares the variable as a string of characters. The interpreter therefore counts the characters, allocates the necessary

```
40  ON ERROR GOTO 8000
200 Q10$ = "IS AN ASSEMBLER A HIGH LEVEL
      LANGUAGE?"
210 Q11$ = " . . . "
220 Q12$ = " . . . "

800 PRINT Q10$
810 GOSUB 5000 :REM* CALLS YES/NO SUBROUTINE*
820 IF FLAG = -1 GOTO 800
      :REM*ANSWER INVALID-ASK AGAIN
830 IF FLAG = 0 PRINT "CORRECT" : GOTO 900
835 REM* IF CORRECT GOES ON TO QUESTION 11
840 IF FLAG = 1 PRINT "YOUR ANSWER IS WRONG"
850 PRINT"THIS IS AN EXPLANATION OF LOW LEVEL
            AND HIGH LEVEL LANGUAGES . . . "

870 GOTO 800 REM* ASK QUESTION 10 AGAIN

900 PRINT Q11$
910 GOSUB 5000
970 REM* AND SO ON

5000 REM*START OF YES/NO SUBROUTINE*
5002 PRINT "(ANSWER YES OR NO)"
5005 INPUT ANSWER$
5010 FLAG = -1 : REM*ASSIGNMENT OF VALUE
5100 IF ANSWER$ ="YES" THEN FLAG=1
5110 IF ANSWER$ ="NO" THEN FLAG=0
5120 PRINT ANSWER$ ,FLAG
      :REM*INTERMEDIATE ANSWER DISPLAYED
5130 RETURN : REM * END OF SUBROUTINE

8000 IF ERL NOT = 5005 GOTO 8030 : REM* ERL IS
      NUMBER  OF LINE IN WHICH ERROR OCCURRED*
8010 PRINT "ENTRY CAUSED ERROR: PLEASE TRY
      AGAIN"
8020 RESUME 5005
8030 PRINT "MALFUNCTION: PROGRAM ABANDONED:
      SORRY"
8040 PRINT "ERROR NO "; ERR; " ERROR LINE "; ERL
8050 END
```

Figure 16. BASIC program

51 consecutive bytes in memory, places the string of characters in memory, and makes an entry in the string variable table giving the variable name, its length and start address.

At line 800 the string *Q10$* is output: in this case it has been moved from the address in the memory of *Q10$* to the display device. It could be moved in a similar way to a line printer or magnetic tape unit, etc.

This program has a large number of questions with yes/no answers, each of which requires the same series of statements to **validate** the answer. The series of statements, therefore, can be placed in a **sub-routine** which can be called from anywhere in the program. After execution of the sub-routine, control is returned to the statement immediately following the one calling it. Here line 810 calls the sub-routine by the *GOSUB* statement. The programmer has added a comment–indicated by the word *REM* for remark–which produces no action, but is printed on the listing of the program as annotation to help anyone changing the program.

At line 5005 the program asks for input from the keyboard; the input routines of the BASIC interpreter accept the characters one by one as keyed. The input when complete is placed in string variable *ANSWER$*.

The program now has to determine whether the answer was yes, no or something else. The sub-routine shown simply compares the content of *ANSWER$* to the strings of characters *YES* and *NO* and sets the content of a numeric variable called *FLAG* to 1 or 0 accordingly, returning the value −1 if the answer is anything other than *YES* or *NO*. This is a simple validation routine, checking before making any further use of the input that it will make sense to the program. The routine could be extended to ignore any spaces or punctuation, to accept upper or lower case letters, to accept the single letters *Y* or *N* alone, and generally to be made more helpful to the user. Some validation is built in to the structure of the language. For example, in BASIC, an attempt to input letters into a variable declared as numeric will be detected by the interpreter.

During program development the programmer may wish to follow the course of the program as it runs. Line 5120 shows a way in which the programmer can add temporary lines, enabling **intermediate results** to be output. In this case the value of the flag is displayed every time the sub-routine is run. The program development package may give the programmer additional aid. For example, a **trace** facility can be used which displays the statement number on the screen and pauses every time a **jump** instruction is obeyed. This allows the programmer to follow the course of the program and find **logical errors**, using **test data**, to ensure that all branches of the program are exercised.

Before reaching the validation sub-routine, the keyboard

input routine may have detected an error. For example, more characters may have been entered than there is space for in location *ANSWER$*. The programmer can set up a routine at line 8000 to be activated when there is an error: during the **initialization**, when the program is first entered, line 40 tells the interpreter to transfer control to line 8000 if it detects any error while running.

If the error occurs while line 5005 is being executed, it is likely that the user can proceed by keying the answer again: the **error routine** therefore resumes operation of the program at line 5005. An error anywhere else results in the program displaying the error condition and then stopping. In an interactive program of this type, substantial effort goes into the writing of error routines to keep the program running wherever possible.

COMBINATION OF PROGRAMS TO FORM SYSTEMS

In a simple case, a **compiled program** is complete in itself, containing all error routines and routines for handling data on external storage devices. A special-purpose computer may even have its program permanently resident in **read only memory**; the program in a pocket calculator is an example of this.

However, to assist the user of a general-purpose computer and to provide efficient use of the equipment, a variety of other programs exists to help generate the program, control its running and its interactions, control the sequence of programs and manage the resources of the system. These programs are known collectively as the **operating system**. This is a term which has changed its meaning over the years. Initially it was used with the particular sense of a system designed to minimize operator actions in running a computer. Later it included all system software, and now it is sometimes used in the narrower sense of a system providing only interception of input/output and management of files on external storage devices.

Control program

An essential concept is that of the control program, also called the **supervisor**, **monitor** or **executive**. In running a single program, data and instructions are passed between the control unit and the memory; the **control register** holds the address of the next instruction to be obeyed. Figure 17 shows a central processor with several programs resident.

A statement in the high level language of Program 1 to 'Read a record from magnetic tape' will have been compiled to 'set up **parameters** of desired record, then call the control program'. The following will then occur.

1. A copy of the Program 1 **registers** and **accumulators** in the control unit will be made to a special area of random access memory.

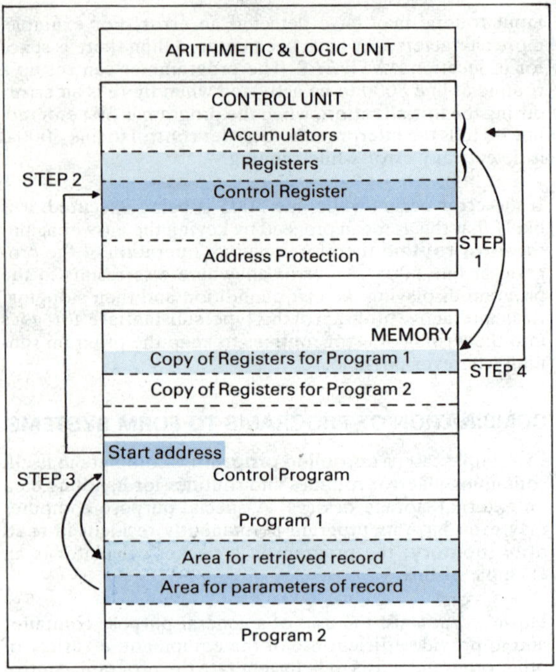

Figure 17. Control program

2. The control program will then be entered by giving the **control register** the address of its first instruction.

3. The control program looks in Program 1 to find what operation is needed, performs it and then puts the retrieved record in an area of memory defined in Program 1.

4. The copy of the Program 1 registers and accumulators is moved back into the control unit. The control register now holds the address of the **next instruction** of Program 1, which continues running.

Multiprogramming is an extension of this procedure. Instead of leaving the processor idle while the comparatively slow movements of the tape drive take place, the control program can allow Program 2 to proceed. If it has been running before, a copy of its registers and accumulators will have been made when it handed over control. This stored copy is moved into the control unit and Program 2 runs until its next call to the control program, or until there is an external **interrupt** which makes the processor restart the control program. Some computers have **address protection** circuits in the control unit to prevent a program accidentally trying to access an area of memory belonging to another program. An extension of the multiprogramming concept allows programs to be running whose total size exceeds the memory–parts of a program can be held on fast external storage devices and brought into memory only when that part is addressed. The techniques of **overlays**, **paging** and **virtual memory** are variants of this.

A major function of the control program is the care of **files** on **external storage devices**. The programmer is aware of a file name and the logical position of a record within that file. The control program keeps a record–in a **directory** on the device–of the physical locations of files. It may make duplicate copies of files for safety, and may deny access if a file is being changed by another program or belongs to another user. A related operation is the **spooling** to the external storage device of slow peripheral input and output. For example, all print data from a program may be diverted to disk and printed some time later when the printer becomes free.

A distinction must be drawn between **data base management systems**, described in Chapter 5, and the **file management routines** of an operating system. In a data base management system the various data items needed by an organization are kept in a single set of files with records related to one another in such a way that any piece of information is kept in one file only. Application programs for the various functions of the organization all use this one set of files. The file management routines of an operating system provide no relationship between the contents of files.

There are various specialized functions which are performed within a computer system – control of disk units, control of telecommunications transfers, performance of special types of numerical calculation. Each of these may have its own processor with its own **dedicated control program**, accessible to the user only through the control program of the central processor.

Sequencing

A complete job, for example invoicing, is carried out by a set of related programs. As each program comes to a stop–completing its task, encountering an error or requiring some external input such as today's date–the operating system initiates the next operation where possible. The steps of the sequence may be set by commands in a **job control language**, prepared by the programmer or operations staff and stored on disk. The job control language is a set of special instructions understood by the operating system designed to guide the computer through the execution of a set of application programs.

Utilities

Some types of program are required for similar manipulations of data in a variety of different applications. Rather than rewriting the programs for each application, utilities or **library packages** are provided as part of the system software. Their running is controlled by the input of parameters, for example the names of files to be copied or the required sequence for sorting.

Generation of programs

The software in this category includes not only the compilers and interpreters which take high level language statements, and convert them to machine code, but also programs which can perform a variety of other functions. These include programs designed to help in the preparation of **flowcharts** and **structuring** of programs, programs which allow the testing of individual modules of large programs, **test data generators** and **report program generators**. Often, the writing and testing of large programs is so complex and expensive that it is economic to provide software to assist this process.

Simulation, emulation and microcode

When a manufacturer introduces a new type of computer or a company changes to a different supplier of computer equipment, there may be a considerable quantity of software written for the old machine which will not run on the new one. To avoid the expense of rewriting programs, it is often desirable therefore to run a program on a computer different from that for which it was written. This can be done in three ways.

1. Simulation Instructions and data are passed through extra electronic circuits by the control unit to convert them to the new form.

2. Emulation This is equivalent to simulation but, in emulation, software is used in the control program to perform the conversion each time an instruction is obeyed.

3. Microcode This is a form of emulation which allows a simple but fast processor with a limited instruction set to obey a more extensive set.

OPERATING SYSTEMS TO SUIT APPLICATIONS

The type of operating system and the range of software in use on a computer are now determined far more by the type of application than by the size of the computer.

A single user doing one job may be helped by multiprogramming and spooling. This would enable, for example, a secretary with a **word processor** to edit one document while the previous one was being printed.

A dentist's office may have a **transaction processing** system–the dentist **updates** the **record** of the patient's teeth after making a filling and the receptionist uses the same files to keep an appointments diary. The same computing principles with very complex software apply to the control of **networks** of thousands of terminals for banks and airlines.

In other systems there are many users each with independent programs and files. **Multi-access scientific computing** is a good example of this. Here, careful safeguards must be implemented to ensure the security of each user's data and programs.

Chapter 4

Information

THE SYSTEMS APPROACH

This chapter provides the basis of knowledge concerning the **nature of information**, its role in organizations and the systems view of organizations. Chapter 5 proceeds to review the way information is represented, arranged, retrieved and processed in computers.

Let us consider a **systems approach** to the solution of problems. The essence of this approach is that in solving a problem it is necessary to think about *all* the relationships and aims of the participants in the problem. If the problem is that chair legs keep breaking, it is not sufficient to provide a stronger material; thinking must also include consideration of the way people sit down. If the problem is that the prisons are full, it is not sufficient to build more prisons; application of the systems approach, asking *why* the people are in prison, also leads to a consideration of probation, community service and other non-custodial sentences. However, asking why prisoners are being punished leads back directly into the conflicts of human values which are least susceptible to solution by the systems approach.

The word **system** has a number of meanings. Summarizing a discussion by Acoff in *Redesigning the Future*, the meaning used here can be defined by the following statements.

1. A system is an *assembly of parts or components* connected together in an *organized way*.
2. The particular assembly has been identified by a *human* as being of *special interest*.
3. In general, the parts are *affected* by being in the system and are *changed* if they leave it.
4. The particular *assembly* of parts *performs some function*.

A number of concepts follow from this definition.

1. The parts perform some function: there must be **input** and **output** flows to and from the system.

2. The performance of these functions must be measurable, which implies **monitoring**.

3. The parts are organized, which implies **control** of actions and a **decision-taking** process.

4. The organization of parts also means that if a part has no interaction or connection with other parts, it is not in the system. The system must therefore have **boundaries**.

5. Beyond the boundaries is an **environment** of objects whose attributes affect or are affected by the system.

6. The system has **resources** available to it.

A number of **sub-systems** exist which interact with each other. There are four categories in particular.

1. The **information** sub-system deals with the flow of information between parts of the system, and between the system and its environment.

2. The **control** sub-system exerts control on the components of the system.

3. The **logistic** sub-system collects resources, and feeds the system with resources.

4. The **process** sub-system provides the functional output from the system.

The division into sub-systems may at other times be into functional sections of an organization; the views of a system change as different aspects are analyzed.

THE ORGANIZATION AS A SYSTEM

Readers of this book will be considering many different types of organization. A review of some of the possible 'input' and 'output' will illuminate the differences: a factory has an input of raw materials and an output of finished goods; a library has an input of money and books and an output of information; a shipping company has an input of goods and delivers an output of the same goods elsewhere. A movie theater may be regarded as an organization with an input of people, and an output of the same people a couple of hours later. Asking how they have been 'processed' raises questions about the nature of entertainment. There is no one methodology which can be applied to the study of all organizations as systems, rather a number of different formal methodologies which are useful in different circumstances as an aid to understanding the interactions of the components in the system.

As an example of the treatment of the organization as a system, Figure 18 shows a steelworks. The **logistics** sub-system provides and pays for materials, transport and men; it also collects money from customers. The **process** sub-system turns the materials into steel of the quality, quantity and dimensions requested. The **information** sub-system takes customer orders, accumulates different orders for similar items, makes a forecast of next month's orders from the trend over the last few months, collects details of the names of the men present so they can be paid correctly and uses customer names and addresses in preparing invoices and delivery routes.

The **control** sub-system turns forecasts into plans, deciding whether to cut production or recruit more salesmen if lower orders are forecast, deciding what steel to make today for stock against the probability of future orders, deciding minute by minute how to cut the steel produced to satisfy orders most economically, steering a crane to pick up a bundle of steel and deciding second by second how to adjust the rolling mill to keep the steel the required size.

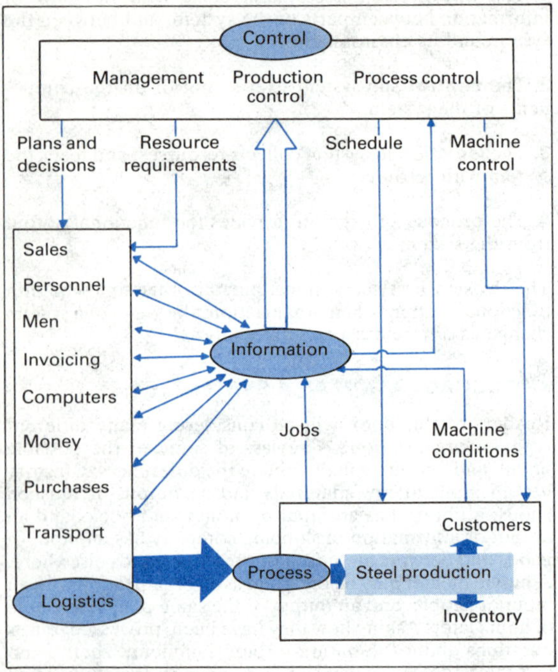

Figure 18. Steelworks as a system

Information and control
The crane driver with an observer form a **control loop** with **feedback**. The driver steers the hook on receipt of a signal, but he must move it slowly enough to enable the observer to make another signal before the hook overshoots the correct place. The speed of control and the speed of information must be matched. This information-control loop is the cybernetic loop of the system. **Cybernetics** is the mathematical science of the transmission and transformation of measurable information, the word being derived from the Greek word for 'steersman'.

Office organization
The office is an information processing system whether or not it uses machines. Office organization can be viewed in two ways. In the first way, the office is viewed as the subsystem which accomplishes the information processing that necessarily accompanies the production process. Figure 19 shows the cycle of this system.

An *order* initiates production and shipping of goods. The

goods are accompanied by a *shipping order* listing them. This list, priced and totalled, is turned into an *invoice*. The customer sends a *check* in payment, and the transaction is completed. Chapter 1 has already considered the progression of machines used to perform the necessary information processing, from **accounting machines**, through to **magnetic ledger cards**, **punched card** systems and **computers**. These tend to take the large-scale processing of accounts out of 'the office' and into 'the data processing department'.

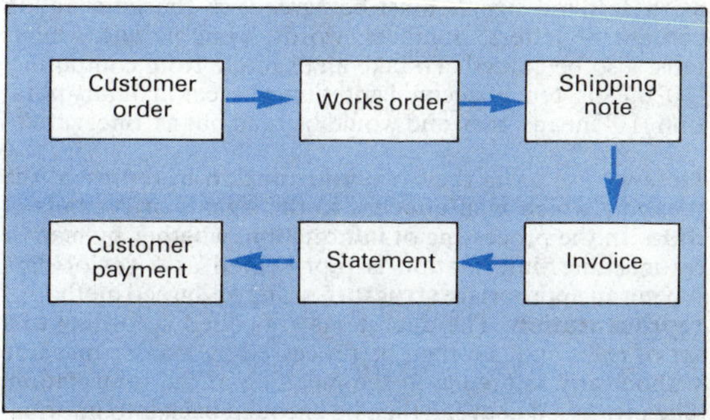

Figure 19. Routine office organization

The second view of office organization is illustrated in Figure 20. This view of the office is more concerned with the *unpredictable* work of the office and the *control functions*. The diagram shows the manager receiving regular information, letters, visitors, phone calls and conducting business outside the office. He obtains information from files, holds discussions with his colleagues, sends out messages and makes decisions. However, the current advances in **microprocessor technology** are increasingly now extending mechanized information processing to the unscheduled work of the office.

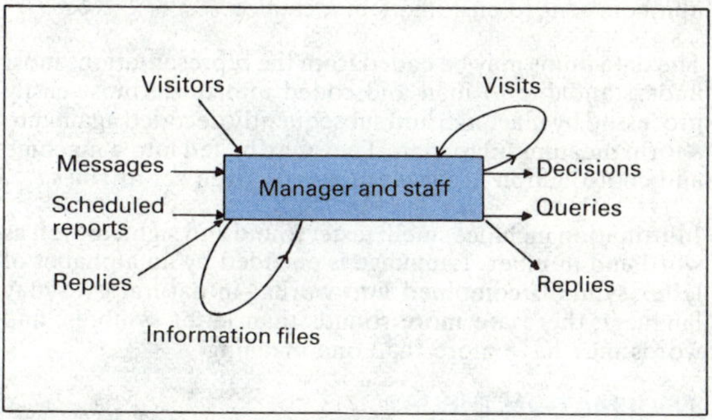

Figure 20. Non-cyclic work of the office

The nature of information

The information flowing around the steelworks took various forms. For example, orders have numbers of items required, dimensions, descriptions, required delivery dates, delivery name and address. They may be given to the firm by letter, telex, telephone or delivered verbally to a salesman.

The crane driver picking up a bundle of steel may be guided by hand signals from a colleague on the ground. They must both first agree on the meaning of the signals–a hand raised may mean 'still too far up' or it may mean 'stop there'. Just as these hand signals must be agreed, so the information content of letters, numbers, words, symbols and sounds must also be agreed. To take an example from computing, '10' means 'ten' in decimal notation whereas in binary notation '10' means 'two' and would be read out as 'one, zero'.

Here we are using the word **information** to represent the meaning which man attaches to the signals or symbols of **data**. In the processing of information, whether by man or by machine, information is represented as a set of data having an appropriate **structure**, using an agreed method of **representation**. The data items are coded according to a set of rules and can then be processed by man or machine without any reference to the meaning of the information. The processed data can then be encoded back into information.

To make the use and flow of information efficient it has to be organized. This organization extends to:

1. Coding and representation;
2. Standards;
3. Structure;
4. Arrangement.

Thus, a list of customers might be arranged alphabetically within geographic regions for the convenience of salesmen, or in account number order for invoicing. Orders may specify steel quality by reference to national standards, government procurement agency standards or the product numbers sent to customers in a catalog.

The data items may be coded from the representations most understandable to man and coded into those most easily processed by machine, and subsequently decoded again into a form meaningful to man. They may be fed into a machine and controlled in accordance with a given set of rules.

Information includes smell, taste, sound and sight, as well as word and number. Language is encoded by an alphabet of letter symbols combined into words–in natural everyday language there are more sounds than letter symbols, and words may have more than one meaning.

INFORMATION THEORY

How much information is flowing in the steelworks of

Figure 18? Information theory provides a basis for answering this question, arguing that any question can be broken down into a number of questions, each with only two possible answers: yes or no; black or white; heads or tails; on or off. The yes/no decision is defined as the smallest unit of information and is called the **bit**, which is a contraction of **binary digit**.

As an example of the number of bits needed to express information, integer numbers from 0 to 31 can be expressed in five bits. A 26-character alphabet can be expressed within five bits. If it is agreed that the question concerns fractions not integers, then 32nds can be coded in five bits, and thousandths within ten bits. The sender and recipient have to agree on the meaning they are giving to the bits; the **precision** with which they can transmit a measurement is determined by the number of bits.

NOT	Negation	A		Result
		0		1
$\overline{A}$	The result is true (1) if A is NOT true.	1		0
OR	**Logical addition**	**A**	**B**	**Result**
		0	0	0
A + B	The result is true (1) if A OR B is true.	0	1	1
		1	0	1
		1	1	1
AND	**Logical multiplication**	**A**	**B**	**Result**
		0	0	0
A.B	The result is true (1) if A AND B are true.	0	1	0
		1	0	0
		1	1	1
	Binary multiplication	**A**	**B**	**Result**
		0	0	0
		0	1	0
		1	0	0
		1	1	1

Summary A	B	Result OR	NOR	AND	NAND	EQ	NEQ
0	0	0	1	0	1	1	0
0	1	1	0	0	1	0	1
1	0	1	0	0	1	0	1
1	1	1	0	1	0	1	0

Table 1. Truth tables

If the information is *numerical,* then combinations of information can be treated according to the rules of **binary arithmetic**. A way of treating the *combination of logical answers* is also needed. The method chosen, in the information theory on which computers are based, is **Boolean algebra**. Like binary arithmetic, this is based on the choice between 'True' and 'False'. All logical operations can be derived from the **AND**, **OR** and **NOT** relationships. Table 1 shows these relationships in words and in the form of truth tables, with 0 for false and 1 for true. The pattern of the logical multiplication table is the same as the pattern of the binary multiplication table, which is convenient mathematically but leads to the inconvenience of the OR relationship being expressed by the '+' symbol, and the AND relationship by the '·' symbol.

The final section of Table 1 adds the **equivalence** operation **EQ**, and the complements **NOR**, **NAND** and **NEQ**; the latter is the **non-equivalence** or **exclusive–or** operation.

This logic can only deal with **truth definite** statements which have the property of being either true or false within the language set in use. An example of a statement which is not truth definite is 'I am lying now'. If the statement is true it is a lie and therefore false.

This discussion has so far dealt with the reduction of information to bits, and the combinations of bits. Information can be coded in various ways. The efficiency of the coding depends on the criteria for efficiency adopted. For example, the Morse code is optimized for the number of bits needed to express a typical sentence in English since the most frequent letters are represented by short codes. E is expressed by '·' and X by '–··–'. For convenience of handling data in computers, however, all character codes are made the same length, and the binary numerical order of letter codes is in alphabetic sequence for ease of sorting and selecting.

If an optimal code is used for transmission, it gives no protection against erroneous information being incorporated during transmission–referred to as **noise**. Additional bits can be added, not to give greater precision but to increase the probability of correct reception. A frequently used system in computer communication is that of **parity**: if seven bits are used to encode a character an eighth is added. For **even parity**, this makes the total number of 1s in the character even, i.e., 0010011 becomes 00100111 with even parity. Conversely, with **odd parity**, 0010011 becomes 00100110, making the total number of 1s odd. This is an error detection code–if the parity bit does not have the correct relationship to the other bits the receiving end asks for a retransmission of the message. With increasing redundancy, error correcting codes can be constructed, giving a finite probability of reconstructing the message after a number of errors.

SOURCES OF INFORMATION

The accuracy of information is closely connected to the way in which it is collected. The main types of question asked are:

1. What has been done?

2. What resources are available?
3. What needs to be done?
4. What is your opinion?

These are arranged in order of ease of mechanization of data collection and information processing.

Automatic data collection may be linked by a **feedback loop** to **automatic control**, for example a thermostat. Data may accompany a product for the express purpose of being collected back again, for example **Kimball tags**, which are miniature punched cards attached to clothing and returned when the garment is sold. Information may be generated on an **exception** basis, for example credit card transactions above a given amount that require authorization.

Any process whereby information in a man's mind is turned into machine-readable data is liable to be subject to errors of understanding and transcription. There are several methods of improving error rates, as given below.

1. Information can be duplicated, giving rise to redundancy of information. Examples include writing the amount in words and figures on checks, double entry book-keeping, the **verification** method of keyboard entry and the use of **check digits** on account numbers.

2. Data can be **validated** by comparison with feasible figures. Examples include rejecting 30 February as a date, querying salaries higher than a certain figure and investigating business taxpayers declaring less than the profit percentage reasonable for their trade.

3. Feedback The data can be shown in legible form to its originator for checking. This includes the proofreading of written matter. It is also advisable for a third party to check the proof since the originator tends to 'see' what was expected, in spite of mistakes being present.

4. Reconciliation Examples include trial balance of double entry book-keeping, cross-totalling, comparison of bank statement with running balance in checkbook and add-listed batch totals on groups of invoices.

5. Turn-around systems can be used which incorporate machine readable data in documents that are sent out from an information processing system. Examples were given in Chapter 2 in the discussion on input devices.

Errors arise even in automatic systems, either through the malfunction of a part or because of the inherent limits of measuring accuracy. Information is not retained indefinitely in the human mind, and so must be captured while fresh. Errors in receipt of information arise from random **noise** or deliberate **encryption** for security. Also, errors may arise because the image in the recipient's mind created by the words used is different from the image in the sender's mind–this problem can be overcome by asking questions that test understanding.

There is nothing new about the occurrence of errors in information. Because computer processing is automatic, it depends on the safeguards built into programs and procedures to try and trap erroneous information, whereas in a paper system errors may be spotted as data is being processed by humans. Once information has been input, it gains credence from the very fact of being in the computer; if, however, a computer system has a reputation for giving wrong information sporadically, all information from it becomes suspect.

Wrong information can originate from mistakes, fraud and misinformation. For example, workers may sign on as 'Mickey Mouse' to avoid taxes, or people may choose to give an age different from their real one to improve their chance of finding a job or a partner.

Standardization of coding

Coding standards may be agreed upon either to reduce uncertainty, e.g., the use of numbered color cards for paint, or to facilitate machine handling, e.g., the use of **product bar codes** on groceries or zip codes for mail.

Types of information

In the steelworks example of Figure 18, information is an adjunct to the main process. There are other organizations where transfers of information form the transactions of the business. Examples include insurance and gambling. In overseas trade, such organizations contribute to 'invisible exports' in which money and information flow but not goods. Other organizations deal in knowledge, i.e. information which is of general applicability rather than being specific to any particular organization.

Quantitative data and statistics

Statistics involves the processing of numerical data to reduce the amount of detail in the data, by obtaining averages and measures of dispersion and correlation. Care must be taken, when applying statistical methods, to ensure that the measure chosen is appropriate for the type of data used, which may be one of the following types.

1. **Nominal**–numbers of named items with no commonality, e.g., 3 dogs, 5 oranges and 7 feathers.
2. **Ordinal**–items with a rank order, e.g., 25 privates, 10 sergeants and 25 generals.
3. **Interval**–items with a unit of measurement common to the list, e.g., Jones 40 votes, Smith 10 votes.

The **mode**, which is the most frequently occurring value, can be applied to all three types of data. The **median**, which is the value such that half the data lie above it and half lie below it, can be applied to ordinal or interval data. The arithmetic **mean**, which is the average number of units, can only be applied to interval data.

Accounting

The flow of money is increasingly being replaced by the flow of information representing money. Accountancy is therefore more concerned with information processing than with actual counting. Monetary dealings between organizations are already almost entirely performed by information transfer, ending with clearing transactions between their respective banks. With the spread of the cashless society, this process is extending to individuals, with pay by credit transfer and purchases by credit card and check.

Forecasting and planning

Forecasting is the prediction of the future based on past results and changes in external influences. One method is by recognizing in data those features that are similar to past events, and making the assumption that history will repeat itself. This method is used in weather forecasting and the chart method of predicting stock market movements. Another method is the statistical analysis of data into a time series, projected forward to predict the future. This forms a simple **mathematical model**, giving an expression of the relationship between variables. **Simulation**, by contrast, is an expression of the reactions between system components, and involves obtaining results by randomizing inputs.

Planning incorporates forecasts which are used to arrive at decisions about future actions considered necessary to produce good results, and sets targets for their achievement by the organization and its sections. Information about the environment, for example about competition and total demand, is required when formulating plans. Once a plan has been set, information on the results can be processed in order to highlight any shortfalls and enable management to pursue action to get back on course.

Chapter 5

Data in Computers

REPRESENTATION

In **binary digital computers,** the smallest element of information is the **binary digit**, abbreviated to **bit**. It is represented by 0 or 1.

Instructions and storage of the central processor may be organized in either **bytes** or **words**. A byte is a fixed number of bits – usually eight – hence the name byte from 'by eight'. A **word** is a collection of bits of length 16, 24, 32, 48, etc., depending on the design of the particular computer. This is defined as the unit of storage and manipulation of data in a particular type of computer.

A **character** is one of the set of symbols that may be represented in a computer. It may be a number, a letter, a mathematical symbol, a punctuation mark or graphics character. Standards for the coding of characters have been developed by national and international standards committees and also by individual manufacturers. A computer may use different codes for the same data as it passes along the steps of a data processing cycle, with code translation between steps. There are four code standards in frequent use.

1. Binary Coded Decimal (BCD) Every four bits represent one decimal digit. Thus two digits can be packed into one 8-bit byte.

2. Extended Binary Coded Decimal Interchange Code (EBCDIC) Every eight bits represent one upper or one lower case letter, symbol or punctuation mark or decimal digit. There are a total of 256 different characters.

3. American Standard Code for Information Interchange (ASCII) This was originally a 7-bit code, similar to EBCDIC but with a different code sequence, and is now an 8-bit code. It incorporates control characters for data transmission and the control of printing, e.g., LF for Line Feed, SOM for Start of Message.

4. International Organization for Standardization 7-bit code (ISO7) This is the same 7-bit code as the first 128 characters of ASCII. Certain codes are designated as being available for national characters – currency symbols and letters with umlauts, accents, etc.

Octal and hexadecimal representation

Sequences of binary digits are unwieldy for people to write, read and remember. For convenience, groups of three bits can be represented by the digits 0 to 7. This is simply a mathematical transposition of numbers from base 2 to base 8, known as **octal**. Alternatively, groups of four bits can be taken; this is convenient as it is half a byte. As there are 16 possibilities the first six letters are needed as well as the decimal digits. This is often referred to as **hexadecimal** representation. Examples of binary, octal and hexadecimal representation of numbers are given below.

Binary	000	001	010	011	100	101	110	111
Octal	0	1	2	3	4	5	6	7

Binary	0000	0001	0010	0011	0100	0101	0110	0111
Hex.	0	1	2	3	4	5	6	7

Binary	1000	1001	1010	1011	1100	1101	1110	1111
Hex.	8	9	A	B	C	D	E	F

Table 2. Octal and hexadecimal digits

Thus, the twelve bits 100110110111 can be represented as 4667 in octal or 9B7 in hexadecimal.

Any binary number can be converted to its decimal equivalent, so the numbers 0 to 255 can also be used to represent the contents of a byte. For example, letter A in ASCII code is 0100 0001, which is 65 in decimal and 41 in hexadecimal.

DATA ITEMS

A data item, representing a meaningful piece of information such as a description or dimension, is held on an external storage device as one or more bytes of information. Information about the name, length, type, meaning and relationship (if any) to adjacent data items is usually contained in the program used to access this data.

The electronic design of the computer provides certain set ways of holding numbers. A **compiler** or **interpreter** uses these to provide the standard methods of declaring number types in the particular language. The programmer chooses the method appropriate to the *precision* and *range* required. As both positive and negative numbers must be represented in a way which allows easy electronic addition and subtraction, binary numbers are usually held in **two's complement** form. In this way a negative number is formed by taking the equivalent positive number in binary, forming the **one's complement** by changing every 0 to a 1 and every 1 to a 0, then adding one to the result. Thus, to form −3 as one byte, 3 is 0000 0011; the one's complement is 1111 1100; the two's complement is 1111 1101. Every negative number has a 1 as the first bit, so the numbers available in one byte are 0111 1111 (+127) to 1000 0000 (−128).

For scientific and accounting applications, greater precision, and a way of representing very small and very large numbers, is needed. A greater degree of precision is obtained by using more bits for the number, and a wider range is obtained by the use of **floating point representation**. In decimal floating point numbers, a **mantissa normalized** to lie in a set range such as 0.1 to 1 is multiplied by the **exponent**, the power of ten to which it is to be raised.

Thus, 0.008, 8 and 8000 would be expressed respectively as:

0.8×10^{-2} 0.8×10^{1} 0.8×10^{4}

The *binary* equivalent system uses *powers of two* as **exponent**. Figure 21 shows a particular implementation used on many microprocessor based systems. The single precision number has three bytes as **mantissa**, forming a signed number normalized so that the implied point precedes it, and a fourth byte, from −128 to +127, is the **exponent**, the power of two by which it is to be multiplied.

Type	Precision	Range	Storage
Integer	Exact if in range	−32768 to 32767	2 Bytes
Double length floating point	55 bits and sign (17 decimal digits)	2^{-128} to 2^{127} (10^{-38} to 10^{38})	8 Bytes
Single length floating point	23 bits and sign (7 decimal digits)	2^{-128} to 2^{127} (10^{-38} to 10^{38})	4 Bytes

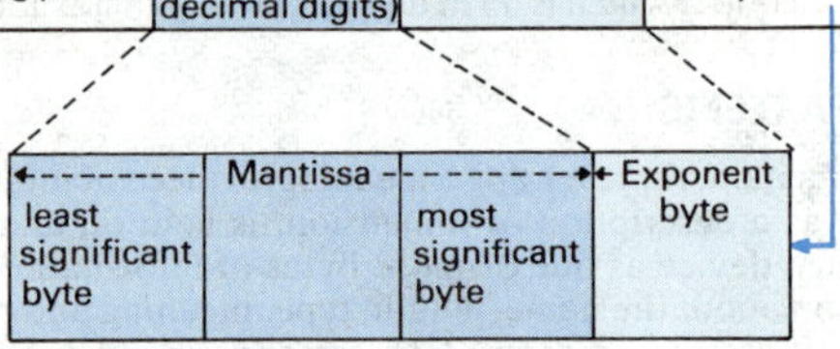

Figure 21. Floating point numbers and precision

Overflow, rounding and truncation

If arithmetic is performed on numbers such that the result cannot be exactly represented by the allocated type of number, one of three things happens. If there is no way of representation, the system will signal an **overflow**, showing that the calculation has failed. For example, 20000 + 30000 cannot be represented or approximated in integer data with a maximum of 32767, and the program will stop. Using **floating point** numbers, results are approximated by **rounding** to the nearest available number or **truncating** by dropping the excess digits. Thus, if 1.0001 and 0.6006 are multiplied using 7-digit precision the result 0.60066006 will be rounded to 0.6006601 or truncated to 0.6006600, depending on the design of the particular computer. Equality tests on floating point numbers should be avoided, since they may fail because of rounding approximations.

In **high level languages** the programmer will not be aware of the details of the binary arithmetic being carried out but must be aware of the precision of the number type in use so that rounding errors are not accidentally introduced. There may be additional information about the data item declared by the programmer. For example, in **COBOL data division** a **variable** may be declared with a **picture** of 999.99, meaning that there are two digits after the decimal point and three before. The COBOL **compiler** makes a table of **variable names** with the length, start address in memory, type and picture listed for each variable. Each time the programmer uses that variable name in a statement the table is used to find the data and to manipulate them correctly.

The meaning of the **variable** is communicated to the outside world by program documentation or headings on reports or displays output from the program. The unit of the variable held with **picture** 999.99 may be meters or millimeters; the programmer has to keep track of the units in use.

Programs as data
Chapter 3 described the operation of **compilers** turning program statements of **source code** into **machine code**. At each stage the program is held and moved about as data. The **statement** in a **high level language** is a **string** of alphanumeric characters and symbols. The **compiler**, which is itself a program, takes this statement string as input and produces **object code** as output. This includes a sequence of numeric **operation codes**, each showing by its form how many succeeding bytes are used by that instruction.

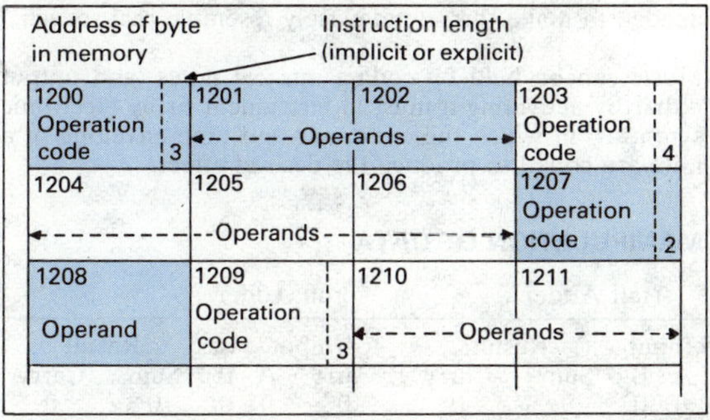

Figure 22. Instructions as data

The succeeding bytes contain **addresses** of data, and for simple **instructions** they may contain the actual **operands**. This **object code**, output onto **external storage** by the **compiler**, can be loaded into the **memory** of the central processor and used to run the program. This can be done any number of times–it does not have to be compiled again each time the program is required.

The object code includes tables of variable names with their addresses and attributes, and tables of program **labels** with their **addresses**. In **multiprogramming** computers, the object code is compiled so that it is **relocatable**: the addresses are given relative to a **base address** which may be altered so that the program can be loaded in different parts of memory depending on what other programs are resident. Thus, the address held in the program is itself a piece of data, manipulated before use.

Pictures as data

The usual way of representing pictures as computer data is to impose a numbered coordinate grid of horizontal and vertical lines. The contents of each rectangle are coded into a character set which may include line elements or solid elements in black and white or color. Alternatively, pictures may be represented by the mathematical formulae of the lines and shapes included or by encoding a library of parts with their dimensions.

Sound as data

Any sound can be analyzed into frequency, amplitude and time distribution; the results can be digitized and the numbers can then be output as speech or music, with reproduction limited by the sampling frequency, precision of holding data and the quality of the sound generation equipment used.

Speech can be held as data by coding a list of words, syllables or *phonemes* which are output in sequence by reproduction from a recording of someone speaking the elements. The application of subsidiary rules for emphasis and pauses is needed to make this sound closely resemble real speech.

Music can be held by coding musical notes, and output either by activating a musical instrument or by electronic synthesis, in which the overtones and time envelope of a note are coded to produce the desired effect.

MANIPULATION OF DATA

Half Adder				Full Adder				
Input		Result		Input			Result	
A	B	Sum	Carry	Carry	A	B	Sum	Carry
0	0	0	0	0	0	0	0	0
0	1	1	0	0	0	1	1	0
1	0	1	0	0	1	0	1	0
1	1	0	1	0	1	1	0	1
				1	0	0	1	0
				1	0	1	0	1
				1	1	0	0	1
				1	1	1	1	1

Table 3. Truth tables for half and full adders

Data are manipulated in digital computers by combinations of **electronic logic gates.** The circuits for **logical instructions** directly implement the relationships set out in Table 1. The **arithmetic circuits** are combinations of these. Table 3 shows the **truth table** for the **half adder,** which adds corresponding bits of two numbers, producing a **sum bit** and a **carry bit**. It will be seen that the sum output is the **exclusive–OR** result and the carry output is the **AND** result. The truth table is also shown for the **full adder**, which takes the **carry** from the previous stage as a third signal in producing its result.

COLLECTIONS OF DATA ITEMS

Stored data items can be referenced by their position in a **multi-dimensional array**; in the two-dimensional case of a table, reference is by row and column number.

	Height (1)	Width (2)	Length (3)
1. Bedroom	2.5	4	3
2. Kitchen	2.5	4	5
3. Living Room	3.5	5	4.5

Table 4. Two-dimensional array

A **variable name** can be allotted to the complete **array**; the program finds the address of a data element from the start address of the array, number of bytes per element and position in the array, as given by **subscript numbers**. Thus, in Table 4, *ROOMSIZE(2,2)* is the width of the kitchen.

The array shown in Table 4 can also be manipulated mathematically as a **matrix** – all figures are dimensions in meters and could be converted to feet by multiplying the matrix by a conversion factor. Some scientific computer languages have facilities for manipulation of matrices.

Elements of an array may contain numbers or character strings, with no connection apart from the convenience of storing them together. In most languages all elements of an array must be the same data type, e.g., all integers.

A **record** is a collection of related data items. The term is particularly used for items input, stored or output together. Thus a punch card record is the 80 characters held on one card. A **field** is a predetermined section of a record, often an individual data item. A **string** is a succession of characters, usually text, held as one data item.

Because the unit which it is convenient to store in one operation on tape or disk is often longer than the convenient collection of data items, **records** are combined into **blocks** for storage or transmission. The **operating system** may control this, the programmer being aware only of individual records.

A **file** is an organized collection of records, normally a set of occurrences of one or more related types of record. The term file can be used for a collection of records in any form, for example a file of enquiries from a terminal or a file as a printed list, but it is most often used for **records** stored on an external device such as a disk drive.

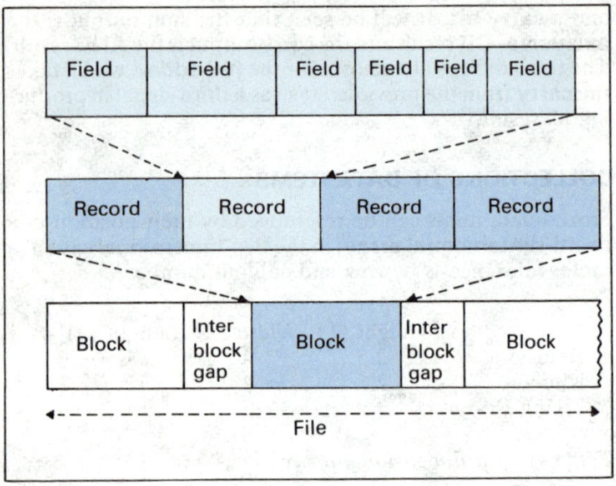

Figure 23. Blocks, records and fields

To allow the file to be organized, one or more fields in the record will be designated to form a **key**; this may be a meaningful field such as an employee's last name and first name, but it is usually an allocated number such as an account number, personnel number, invoice number, insurance policy number, social security number or a serial number for a transaction.

FILE ORGANIZATION

In describing the common file organizations the following processing will be used as an example. A **master file** contains records having keys 1, 2, 4, 6, 9, 16, 23, 39, 57. Transactions arise which require the addition of record 12, a change to record 23 and the addition of record 7 to the file.

Serial and sequential files

As shown in Figure 24, these transactions as they arise can be accumulated in a **serial** file. The records in this file are held one after the other in an order not related to their keys, for example in order as received. The file is completed by an **end of file** record. Records in a serial file may not even have any keys – they could contain successive paragraphs of text.

In a **sequential** file, records are held one after the other in order of their keys. Figure 24 shows the accumulated records of the serial file **sorted** into a sequential file. The procedure to process this is as follows. The first transaction record 7 is read, and held on **disk storage**. Records 1, 2, 4 and 6 of the **master file** are read, and copied to an **updated master file**; the new record 7 is then added. Transaction record 12 is read, and again records are copied across until 12 can be added. The process described so far is the **merging** of two **sorted files**. For the next transaction, record 23 exists in both files: the change indicated by the transaction record is applied to the master record, and the revised record is written to the new file. This proceeds to the end of both files.

Serial and **sequential files** can be held on either **serial** or **direct access storage devices**: the **merging** and **updating** procedure described is typical of a **magnetic tape** system.

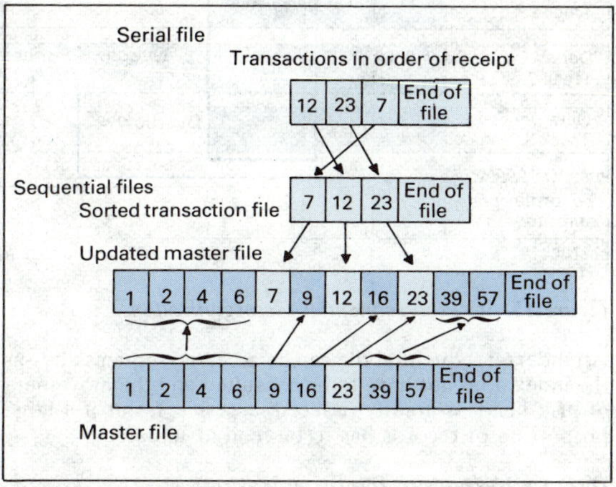

Figure 24. Serial and sequential file organization

Indexed sequential file organization

Figure 25 shows the same transactions being processed against an **indexed sequential** file, which is the most common organization of files on **direct access** disk storage devices. The records are initially arranged sequentially on the disk, leaving part of each **track** empty for later additions. An **index** is then formed and stored on a special track, listing the highest **key** numbers on each track. To read a record, the application program instruction may be as simple as *GET RECORD 23*. By reading the index, the **file management routine** of the operating system discovers that records over 16 and up to 57 are on track 3. It therefore reads each record on that track until it finds one with key 23.

When it comes to add record 12, there is room in the **overflow area** of track 2. However, this fills the track and so record 7, which should also go on Track 2, is placed on a **secondary overflow** track. The number of the overflow track is placed in a **pointer record** on the home track, so that a subsequent search of track 2 looking for record 7 will be continued there.

This organization is very flexible because it is not necessary to know in advance how the keys are distributed. Changes and additions can easily be made. However, if many records are in secondary overflow areas, access can become slow. The file is therefore reorganized periodically into its correct sequence.

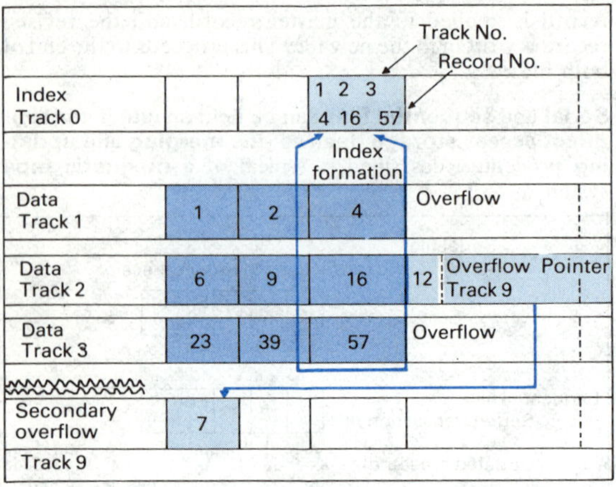

Figure 25. Indexed sequential file organization

An indexed sequential file can be accessed sequentially–as the index does not have to be consulted and the movement of disk heads is greatly reduced, access is faster if a large proportion of records has to be read or updated.

Direct and random file organization

Like many terms in computing, the phrases **direct access** and **random access** are used with several meanings. In the first meaning, they are synonymous and apply to any form of **immediate access storage device** in which a stored record can be retrieved and replaced without reading or copying all others before it. The phrases also have distinct meanings as applied to file organization. In **direct** organiza-

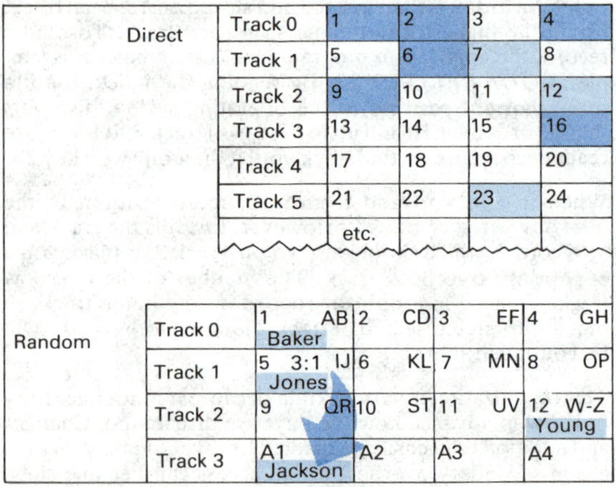

Figure 26. Direct and random file organization

tion, there is a separate space on the disk for every possible **key number**. This organization is simple and quick in operation, as there are no index records or overflows, but it can be very inefficient in its use of disk space. Figure 26 shows a file being accessed **directly**, with addition of records 7 and 12, and a change to record 23.

In the **random** organization, an address is calculated from the key but there are substantially more possible keys than addresses. Figure 26 shows an example in which the address is generated from the initial letter of the surname. If Baker, Young, Jones and Jackson try to occupy their correct addresses, Jackson finds address 5 already occupied by Jones. She therefore has to sit in the overflow area, leaving a notice pinned up at 5 to say where she has gone.

Searching methods

If a **sequential** file is stored on a **direct access** device, records can be accessed by a **binary search**, as shown in Figure 27. The record physically halfway along the file is accessed; the search is then made forwards if that key is lower than the one sought, backwards if higher, halving the proportion of the file skipped on each step until the right track is found.

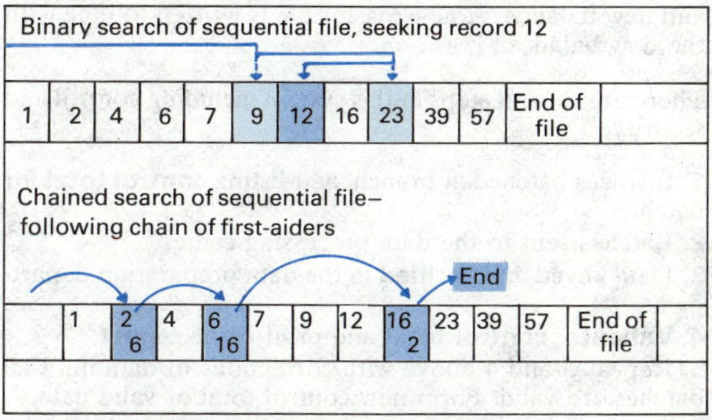

Figure 27. Binary search and chained search

Techniques of **lists** and **chained files** can be applied to any direct access organization. These techniques are commonly used in database organization. As an example, take a personnel file on which one attribute recorded is a first aid qualification. To access records of first aiders, a separate **list** can be kept of the key numbers of their records. Alternatively, using the **chained file** technique, shown in Figure 27, the record for each first aider contains as a **pointer** the **key number** of the next one in the file, with the last one pointing back to the first. A separate file will hold the first key number for each attribute.

Finding a file

Before accessing records, the correct file has to be found. Each tape or disk should have a number unique within the installation, recorded magnetically in a tape header or disk systems area, and written visibly on the outside. The computer installation will have a paper or computer-held register of applications, file names and serial numbers. In a large installation the operating system will keep complex directories of files and media.

DATA PROCESSING AND CONTROL

The processing of the repetitive data of business may involve batch processing, preceded by collection and sorting of data for a period and followed by distribution of results, or it may be on-line with transactions processed as they arise and with resultant actions performed immediately in real time.

Batch processing

Figure 28 shows in flowchart form the elements of a **batch processing** system, using a monthly sales ledger as an example. The month's sales transactions are sorted by customer number onto a magnetic tape. This is processed together with the master file. For each customer in sequence the balance owing from last month is retrieved, updated with this month's payments and purchases, and a statement is printed for the customer showing the detail transactions and new balance. A new master file is written to tape with the new balance.

There are several steps in this system including control and security.

1. Invoices batched at branch, add-listing **control total** for batch.
2. Batches sent to the data processing center.
3. Data keyed and **verified** in the data preparation department.
4. Validate, **control total** and print **error report**.
5. Repeat 3 and 4 above with corrections to data until all batches are valid. Form new control total of valid data.
6. Payments data from accounts department keyed as 3, 4, 5 above.
7. Take **security** copy of all input tapes.
8. Sort input in customer **key** order.
9. Update balances, print customer statements and form **control totals** of processing run.
10. Release output if controls are correct–otherwise find error and re-run as necessary.
11. Security copy of new master file and input file taken off site.
12. Release previous **grandfather** file.

The master file input to a processing run is termed the **father**, the master file generated is the **son**, and the input to the previous run is the **grandfather**. By keeping the grandfather and the transaction input from the previous run, the run can be repeated if necessary.

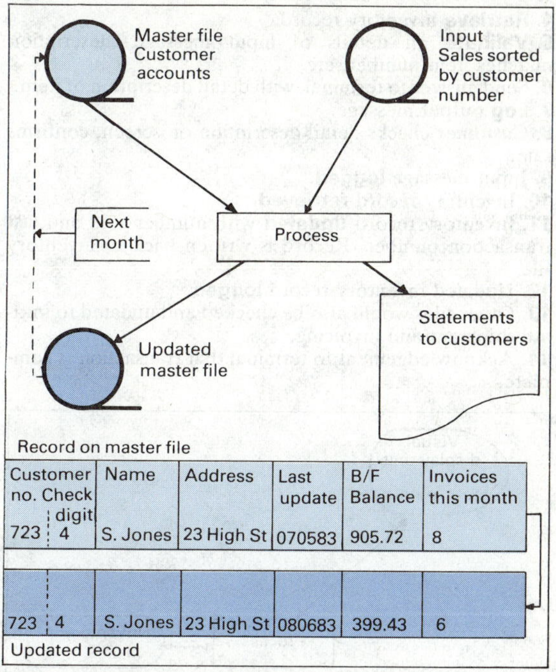

Figure 28. Batch processing

In **transaction processing** the individual inputs are processed as they arise. The **validation** process has to be more thorough as there is no opportunity to correct the input later. The input may never have existed as a paper document. For example, the details of an order may be input directly into a **terminal** by a customer sitting at home. Once it has entered the system, a transaction and the files it affects must be kept secure.

Security and control can be divided into two parts–those occurring during transactions and those done as a batch processing run at intervals, for example at the end of the day. There are many ways of implementing security in **real time** systems; the hypothetical system described here is intended to bring out key points, not all of which would be combined in a real system.

The **transaction processing** phase includes the following procedures.

1. Inquiry from terminal: can you supply ten bracelets, item 2976?
2. Input message **logged** as received, transaction number allocated.
3. Validate check digit on item number.

4. Retrieve inventory record.
5. Validate all details of input message – description matches item number, etc.
6. Send answer to terminal, with detail description of item.
7. Log output message.
8. Customer checks detail description on screen, confirms sale.
9. Input message **logged**.
10. Inventory record **retrieved**.
11. Inventory record **updated** with number sold and last transaction number. Record is written back to inventory file.
12. Updated inventory record **logged**.
13. Other files would also be checked and updated to initiate shipment and invoicing.
14. Acknowledgement to terminal that transaction is complete.

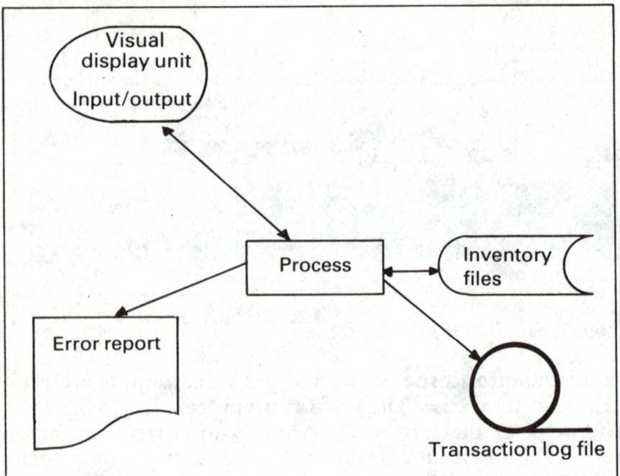

Record before this transaction

Item no. Check digit		Item	Price	Physical inventory	Inventory allocated	Last trans. no.	Transactions today
297	6	Bracelet	2000	300	15	152	3
297	6	Bracelet	2000	300	25	175	4

Record after this transaction

Figure 29. Transaction processing

The **batch processing** phase of the transaction system includes the following procedures.

1. Copy end-of-day inventory file.

2. Input discrepancies from physical inventory check and print report.

3. Shipments and receipts runs also accumulate totals of items shipped and received–compare **control totals** from different runs.

4. Compare control totals for day; if incorrect, use **error** and **transaction logs** to find and correct discrepancies.

5. Create **master inventory file** for tomorrow. Take **security copy** to fireproof safe.

The control is:

1. Within one system, keeping track of transactions and files.

2. Between different systems, comparing today's sales with tomorrow's warehouse shipping list.

3. By physical check of inventory in warehouse–to detect theft and mistakes and keep the computer record in line with actual stock.

4. By keeping logs of all transactions available for making corrections or for audit.

DATABASES

The description of processing so far has related to **files** containing **records** of the *same format;* items may have variable length and there may be a variable number of repeats of items within a record, but the basis is the same. To find a record, it is necessary to use the **key** by which the file is physically organized.

In a **database** it is possible to *retrieve data in more than one way,* without necessarily having to know the key or search the whole file.

This is achieved by putting another layer of software, the **database management system**, between the user and the data. The data are stored together with additional **indexes** and information on the **relationships** between the data items.

There are two views of the advantages of a **database**.

1. Information retrieval To select data items with certain characteristics and output, a formatted report can be compiled using a **query language**, without having to write special applications programs.

2. Data processing Data for the whole organization are stored in a coherent fashion with common definitions and in a number of databases. Within a database, data items can be added and application programs can be developed to process data in a new way, without changing the original applications programs or their view of the data.

The **data dictionary**, which can apply to a number of databases in an organization, lists names of data items with their definitions and characteristics. One organization is likely to have a number of different databases – for example, a local authority may have one for books in its libraries and another for buildings in its area. It is advisable to use one data dictionary so that *LIBRARY* is agreed to mean the building and not the stack of books, but data relationships for the two purposes are so different that putting all information in one database would cause unnecessary complication.

A **schema** is a map of the overall logical structure of a database, including all data items contained in the database. A **subschema** is a map of the logical structure of those data items in a database used by a particular suite of applications programs. Figure 30 shows the relationships of two subschemas to a schema.

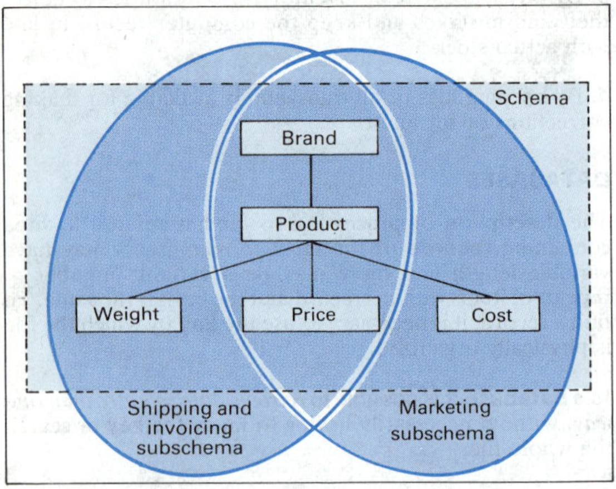

Figure 30. Schema and subschema

The organization now needs a person to look after the **schema** and **data dictionary** – a **database administrator**. This person has two additional responsibilities.

1. Data integrity It is necessary to make sure people don't put nonsense into the system.

2. Data security It is important to ensure that only authorized people can access data, and that data in the system does not accidentally disappear.

Database types

1. Multi-indexed, chained or inverted files

The use of chains and lists has already been described earlier in this chapter. In an **inverted** file, a number of **lists of keys** are kept, each ordered according to one of the variables in the record. For example, a trucking company might keep a file of trucks in license number order, with the file **inverted** by load length, tonnage and fuel consumption. The vehicle which can most economically carry a 6-meter load weighing 5 tons can be found very quickly by running up all three lists until a match is found.

2. Hierarchical database

A hierarchical database is a collection of a variety of types of record with a defined *relationship* between records, at different *levels* of a structure. The simplest case is the **tree structure**, shown in Figure 31. The words used to define the **elements** or **nodes** of this are a mixture of family and tree terms. One **parent** can have a number of **children**, who in turn can be **parents** of **children** at lower levels of the tree. The highest level is the **root**, and a **node** with no **children** is a **leaf**. In a **tree structure** a **child** can have only one **parent**.

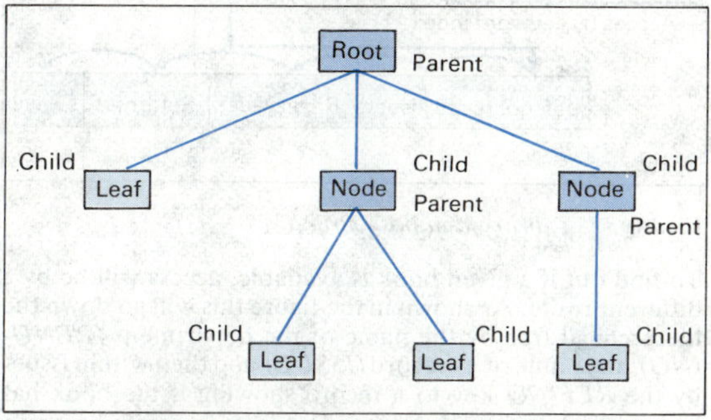

Figure 31. Tree structure

The type of structure in which a child can have several parents is termed a **network** structure. Any **network structure** can be broken down into a number of **tree structures**. Although the structure then has to be drawn with a particular node appearing in several trees, the physical data are held once only, the structure being defined in statements of a **data description language**.

There are a number of **database management systems** based on hierarchical structures. Like programming languages, some have been defined by equipment manufacturers and software houses, others by committees. **CODASYL**, the committee responsible for the language **COBOL**, have defined a set of database standards to extend the language.

The formal statement of the structure of a hierarchical database defines the connections between records and their keys, and the ways in which records can be accessed.

Figure 32 shows a library database. One access method is through an indexed list; for example **keywords** in the book title may be indexed. Thus, if a book on *cybernetics* is required, which may appear with business computers, industrial control systems, mathematics or linguistics, an initial inquiry may be made through a keyword. This will give a list of books with locations and reference numbers.

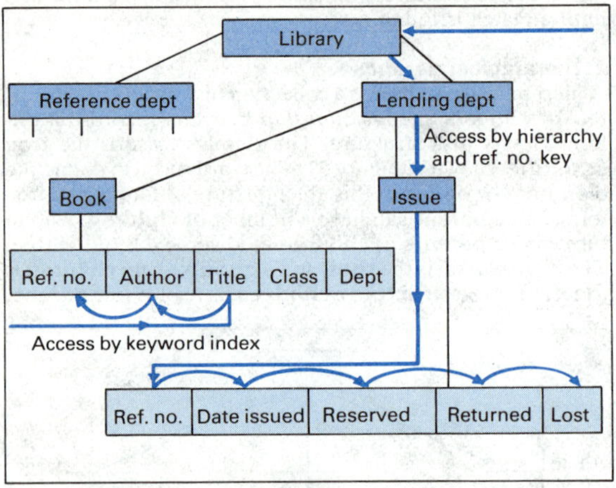

Figure 32. Library database structure

To find out if a given book is available, access will be by a different route. As shown in the figure this will go down the hierarchical tree by the name of the department *(LENDING)*, the name of its record *(ISSUE)* and then within issues by the *REF-NO* key to a record showing if the book has been issued, reserved, returned or lost.

This database and access are structured so the database can be **distributed**–the issue records are kept in the lending library on a small computer which is linked to a central computer holding the classified records of books with indexes of keywords and authors.

3. Relational database
A relational database reduces all data to two-dimensional **tables** in which the order of rows and the order of columns is immaterial, and in which the record occupying a row has a unique key. The reduction of data to this form is termed **normalization**. Hierarchical structures are complicated to draw and amend, and difficult to comprehend; relational databases are simple to comprehend and have recently been widely developed on microprocessor based systems.

Thus, Table 5 shows restaurant items and the relations between them are expressed as:

1. *MENU* table, which is keyed on *ITEM-NO* and *CONSTITUENT-NO,* also contains *QUANTITY.*
2. *ITEM* table, keyed on *ITEM-NO,* also contains *NAME* and *CATEGORY.*

Thus a steak meal (1) includes a salad plate (4), which is a quarter of a salad recipe (8), which includes two tomatoes (6) as ingredients.

MENU			ITEM		
Item no.	Constituent no.	Qty	Item no.	Category	Name
1	2	1	1	Meal	Steak meal
1	4	1	2	Dish	Steak & fries
1	5	1	3	Ingred.	Steak
8	6	2	4	Dish	Salad plate
8	7	1	5	Ingred.	Apple pie
8	10	1	6	Ingred.	Tomato
4	8	0.25	7	Ingred.	Lettuce
2	9	4	8	Recipe	Salad
2	3	1	9	Ingred.	Fries
			10	Ingred.	Dressing

Table 5. Relational database.

Chapter 6

Systems Analysis

This chapter first describes two methods of the communication of logical solutions–decision tables and flowcharts. It then describes the stages of analysis, design and implementation of a system.

DECISION TABLES

It is sometimes convenient to list all the possible conditions, and the action to be taken on every possible combination of conditions, in a decision table.

Grant level procedure									
Conditions	Rules								
	1	2	3	4	5	6	7	8	9
Live at home	Y	Y	Y	N	N	N	N	N	N
Married	Y	Y	N	Y	N	N	Y	–	N
Over 21	Y	N	–	–	Y	N	–	Y	N
Live in college	–	–	–	N	N	N	Y	Y	Y
Actions									
Grant level 1		X	X						
Grant level 2	X					X			X
Grant level 3				X	X				
Appeal possible if hardship	X	X							
Query procedure							X	X	

Figure 33. Limited entry decision table

Figure 33 is a decision table with a set of rules for determining student grants. There are three levels of grant, depending in various combinations on whether the student lives at home, is married and is over 21 or, for single students under 21 only, lives in college accommodation. The table is divided into four sections.

1. **Condition stub**, top left, listing the possible conditions.
2. **Action stub**, bottom left, listing the possible actions.
3. **Condition entry**, top right, arranged to give a column for each possible combination of conditions.
4. **Action entry**, bottom right, showing which actions apply to each column.

This **limited entry** form of decision table makes it very easy to see that all conditions have been considered, and that all listed actions have a means of entry. In the condition entry in Figure 33, *dashes* have been used in two circumstances: in cases where the answer is immaterial, such as the answer to 'Over 21?' for rules 3 and 4; and in cases where the answer is determined by a previous response, for example 'Live in college?' when 'Live at home?' has already been answered with 'Yes'. The number of conditions represented by dashes must be counted carefully to ensure the table is complete.

An **extended entry** decision table is similar, but allows the condition entry to contain part of the condition, and the action entry to contain part of the definition of the action. Figure 34 shows, as an extended entry decision table, conditions for a thermostat program; this is given later in flowchart form in Figure 37.

THERMOSTAT				
CONDITION	Rule 1	2	3	4
Measured temperature	<2°	2 or over and <T	>T+1	Else
ACTION				
Freezing alarm	X			
Set heater	On	On	Off	No change
Wait 5 seconds remeasure temperature	X	X	X	X

Figure 34. Extended entry decision table

Software is available which can construct programs from decision tables, normally as a decision table pre-processor which generates statements in a high level language.

FLOWCHARTS

A flowchart is a form of diagrammatic representation of the processing of information in a system. There are *standard symbols* for drawing flowcharts. A basic set uses general symbols for input, output and storage. Note that these symbols, with suitable annotation, are always sufficient: some authorities prefer to standardize on these symbols only. There are additional specific symbols which represent the type of input, output and storage.

Flow lines are assumed to go from top to bottom and left to right unless the direction is shown by arrows. In a systems flowchart, several lines can enter or leave an operations box.

In any flowchart, clarity is paramount. Comment can be added, and symbols can be numbered to correspond to other documentation. Flowlines should not cross each other: it is better to use connector symbols.

A **data**, or **system, flowchart** shows the overall flow of a system including computer, clerical and management procedures. The example in Figure 35 is a credit reference system, using general symbols for input.

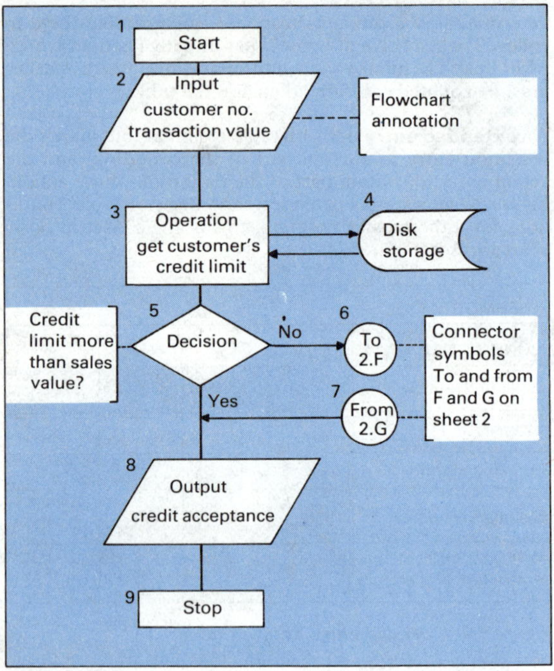

Figure 35. System flowchart, using general symbols

1. Start symbol.
2. Input or output symbol: input.
3. Symbol for **operation**.
4. Symbol for any **on-line storage**.
5. Decision symbol.
6. Connector, labelled F, to a management procedure on another sheet which either gives or refuses credit.
7. If accepted, flow returns to this sheet at connector G.
8. Input/output symbol: output acceptance.
9. Stop symbol.

The example in Figure 36 is a system for marking multiple choice examinations using specific symbols. In addition to those used here, symbols are available for paper tape, communications link, magnetic drum, visual display unit and others.

The following is a list of special symbols used in Figure 36.

1. Input of documents: the **document** symbol is repeated to show there is a large number.
2. Punched card symbol: input parameters.
3. Operation symbol: marking routine.
4. Manual operation symbol: lecturer allocates marks for documents which were rejected by reading machine.

5. Terminal input symbol: manually assessed marks entered.
6. Disk storage symbol: files of correct answers and student marks.
7./8. Operation symbols: merge, sort by student number.
9. Magnetic tapes: archive of results.
10. Document symbol for printed output: results list.

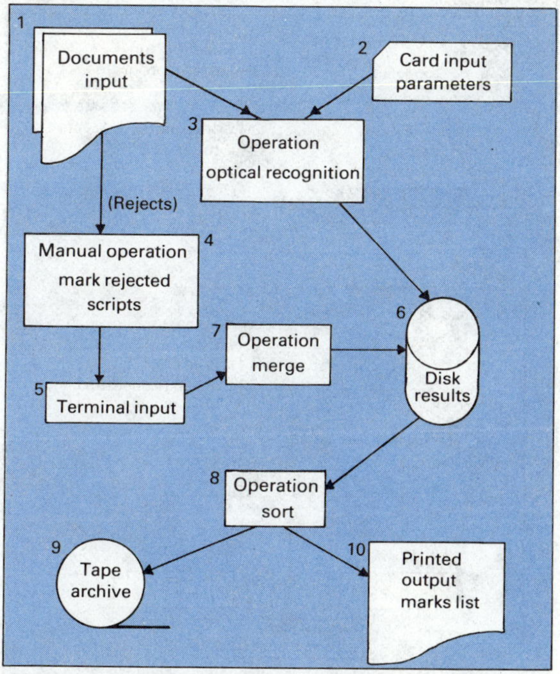

Figure 36. System flowchart with specific symbols

In a program flowchart, the symbols used are the same as those in the system flowchart, usually with general symbols only. The flowchart is more detailed, representing the **algorithms** to be used. An operation box in a program flowchart can have only one line entering it and one leaving it. A decision box can have two or three lines leaving from corners, or one line leaving with branches for any number of possible conditions. Flows combine by the joining of flow-lines, not by a number of lines entering a box.

The example shown in Figure 37 is a thermostat control system.

1. The desired temperature is set.
2. The temperature is measured.
3. Jump if temperature is near freezing.
4. Alarm procedure; the symbol shows a **procedure**

detailed on another flowchart which is most often used for a **sub-routine** in a program.

5. Decide if the temperature is outside a 1 degree band.

6. Switch on heater if low.

7. Switch off heater if high.

8. Wait five seconds so that the heater is not switched on and off too rapidly, then jump back to step 2 and repeat the loop.

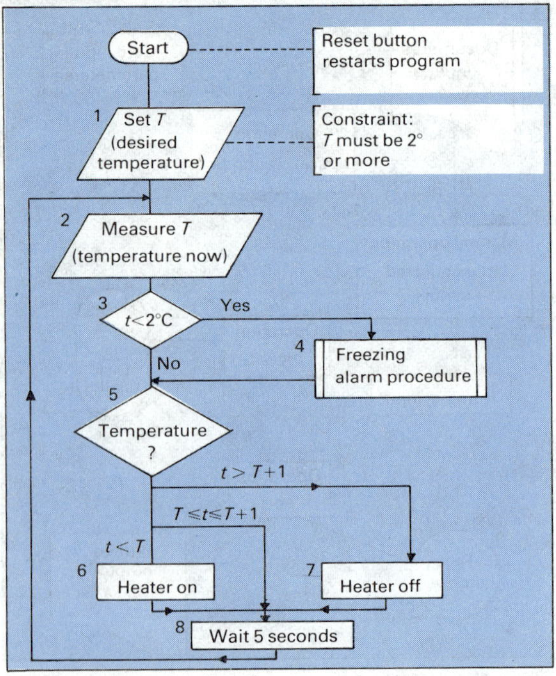

Figure 37. Program flowchart

ANALYSIS OF PROBLEMS AND DEVELOPMENT OF SOLUTIONS

The steps of **investigation**, **analysis** and **design** proceed in cycles of increasing detail, each cycle culminating in a report. Before proceeding to describe these, the basic steps of a **solution** and its **logical statement** will be described. The analysis process involves finding out what information is input, how it is processed – i.e. what decisions are taken and how it is output. If the problem is one with no current method of solution, a precise definition of the problem will have to be constructed and the requirements of the solution identified.

As an example of the solution process, consider a student, John, who has been admitted to various colleges on the basis of his examination grades in physics, mathematics and chemistry. The offers are shown in Table 6, on page 78.

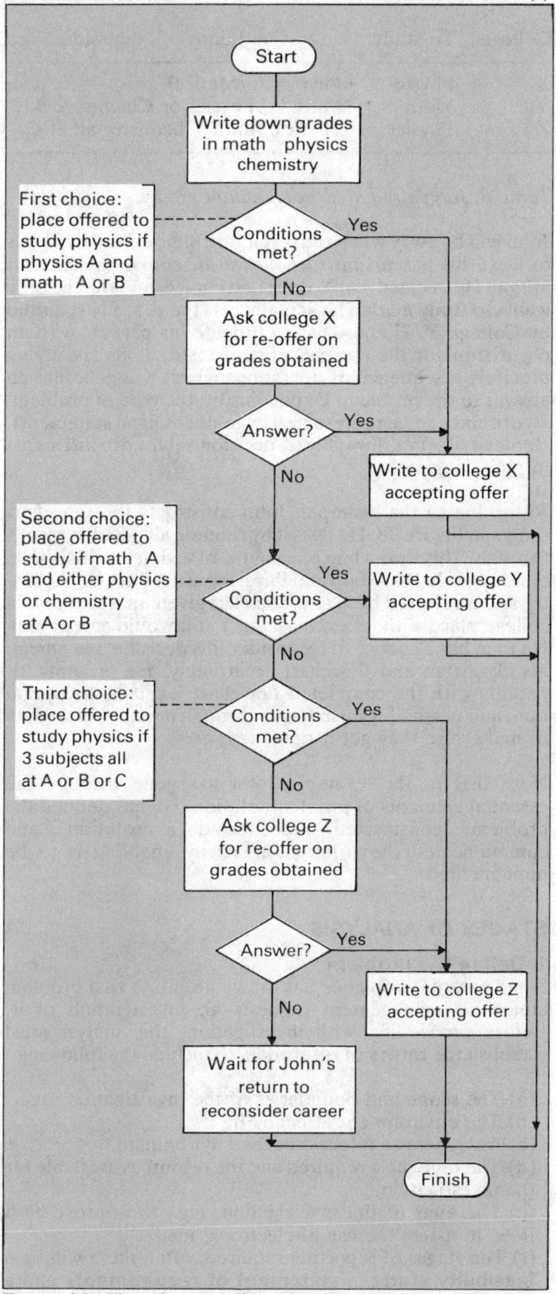

Figure 38. Flowchart of algorithm for choosing a college

College	To study	Conditions of admission
X	Physics	Physics A, Math B.
Y	Math	Math A, Physics or Chemistry B.
Z	Physics	Physics, Math, Chemistry all at C.

Table 6. John's required examination grades

John will be away when the results are announced, so he has to leave his parents *instructions on the course of action to follow.* He decides that X is his first choice, and that he only wants to study math if he actually gets the A grade required by College Y. He now has to provide his parents with an **algorithm** for the choice: a list of instructions specifying precisely a sequence of operations which will generate an answer to the problem. Depending on the type of problem, algorithms can be represented by mathematical statements, Boolean algebra, flowcharts, decision tables or statements in plain language.

Returning to the example, John constructs the flowchart shown in Figure 38. He tests it by running all possible results through. This shows him one course of action in which, if he obtains grade B in Math and Physics but a failure in Chemistry and is rejected by X and Z, he has given up a chance of a college place without even asking Y if it would accept him. He then has a chance to reconsider this decision and amend his algorithm and flowchart accordingly. He presents his parents with the completed flowchart, explains its operation, and persuades them to run through it with sample data to make sure they get it right.

Note that in this example John has gone through the essential elements of problem solution. He has defined the problem, constructed and tested a solution, and communicated the solution in a way enabling it to be implemented.

STAGES OF ANALYSIS

1. Define the problem

Some external influence has drawn attention to a problem area, and management requests an investigation of it. Before proceeding with investigation, the analyst must establish the **terms of reference**, to include the following.

(a) The scope and boundaries of the investigation area.
(b) The environment affecting it.
(c) Any changes forecast in the environment.
(d) The time scale required and the resources available for the investigation.
(e) The aims of the investigation, e.g., to improve cash flow, to assess the use of electronic mail.
(f) The stages of reporting required; often these will be a **feasibility study**, a **statement of requirements** and a **detailed system design**.

Once the problem has been defined and terms of reference established, a feasibility study is undertaken.

2. Feasibility study

Fact finding will be at a general level. For example, it might produce the following type of statement. 'Four clerks are employed full time on the maintenance of inventory records; reports to management on the value and turnover of inventory take three weeks to prepare; telephone queries on the level of stock of a particular item are answered within a minute by clerks consulting card records.' *Objectives* will have been stated in the terms of reference but will be restated and amplified: in particular, the strengths of the present system as well as its weaknesses will be highlighted. A *solution* will be proposed, with its costs and benefits and a discussion of alternatives. It may become apparent from the wider view of the system approach that the boundaries of the problem, as stated in the terms of reference, are not appropriate in the light of the business aims of the concern, and a change in the terms of reference may then be negotiated.

The result of the feasibility study will be a report for management. Many types of recommendations might be made. For example, a recommendation to pursue a more detailed study, to pursue improvements but not using computer methods, not to proceed or to wait for the completion of computer plans for some other department which would provide input, might be made.

The feasibility report will be discussed and amended until a decision is taken on whether to proceed. The *management review* of the feasibility study will include consideration of the effect on staff, possibly with commencement of staff consultation and negotiation.

ANALYSIS AND DESIGN OF USER FACILITIES

In this stage the present system and requirements of the new system are analyzed in detail. Solutions are discussed and one chosen, to the extent that:

1. The user facilities are defined in detail;

2. The **hardware** and **software** requirements are specified in sufficient detail to choose suppliers if necessary, and prepare implementation plans and contracts.

This phase will include fact finding and analysis.

Fact finding

This involves establishing the details of what work is done and what decisions are taken, by whom, when and where. It must include not only the routine flow of work but the treatment of exceptions, errors and inquiries, and details of how the work changes at year end, holidays and peak periods. The system being investigated will be one of information processing, so the facts to be found are the details of input, processing, storage and output.

There are five **main techniques of fact finding** as listed below.

1. The formal *record of present procedure* is inspected. The record may consist of external documents such as statutory requirements and standards, or it may be documentation prepared within the concern, setting out the way procedures are intended to operate. It provides the essential skeleton for fact finding.

2. Interviews and **record collection** are the most frequently used and most effective method of acquiring information on what is actually done, as opposed to what is supposed to be done. Each interview should be prepared in advance, with a list of information to be obtained, but the interview must be allowed to diverge from the plan to discuss other relevant aspects of which the analyst was unaware. Copies of documents and records with information entered must be obtained, both by obtaining examples at interviews and by sampling past records at random. Legible notes of the interview must be made at once. Following an interview, points can be clarified in telephone conversations. Information obtained in interviews can be confirmed by sending a copy of the notes.

3. Questionnaires are valuable where a large number of branches or outside contacts are involved, but their use needs careful consideration as recipients find them a nuisance to answer. They may, of course, be sent to a sample of contacts.

4. Making a group of experienced user department staff an integral part of the study team is a valuable method. It may involve taking staff away from their normal duties for a period, or the formation of a panel of staff members to meet at intervals, initially to provide information and later to comment on the effects of proposed solutions.

5. Observation is most likely to be in addition to interviewing. It may be necessary in establishing information such as the rate of arrival of customers and the length of time taken to serve them, using techniques of work study.

Analysis

Chapter 4 introduced the systems approach. This uses the concepts of boundary, environment, input, output and process.

Logically, analysis follows fact finding. In practice, the two must overlap since it is only by analyzing facts that gaps can be found in the information collected.

There are a number of *systematic methods of analysis*, some of them linked to the design and programming methods to form a coherent whole. A particular data processing department may choose to use one of these methods as its standard.

Systematic methods include:

1. Top-down structured analysis The system under investigation is broken down by stages into smaller subsystems, overall functions being established and documented before details of procedure are analyzed.

2. Information flow diagrams A chart is drawn showing every person and department involved in the system, and all the formal and informal information flows between them. The flows are analyzed to ascertain whether they are needed, before proceeding to the design stage.

3. Precedent The documentation or experience of a similar system previously developed is used as a standard starting point, and the analysis establishes the equivalents to the components of the standard, and the differences between the standard and the system under investigation.

4. Performance analysis This is particularly useful in examining an existing computer system with a view to updating it. Several aspects need to be investigated: a critical examination of the good and bad points of the system from the viewpoint of the facilities provided to the users; the computer resources used by the system; and the costs and benefits achieved by the system.

Systems design

The design of a new system extends to clerical procedures and all ancillary operations as well as the design of the computer system itself.

This is the problem solution phase. Facts have been collected and analyzed. It is now necessary to construct the logic of a set of procedures to perform the operations needed, and also to decide on what computer those procedures will run, what methods of input and output will be used, and what information must be held in files.

Systems design is usually a compromise, arrived at after a consideration of the following factors.

1. Aims of the enterprise.

2. Needs of the user.

3. Statute, audit, other external requirements.

4. Data processing strategy of the enterprise.

5. Cost benefit analysis.

6. Interfaces to other existing or planned systems.

7. Requirements of the particular system as revealed by fact-finding and analysis, including reliability requirement and time constraints.

8. Predecessor system, minimizing change and making use of existing procedures where appropriate.

9. New technology: consider options of hardware, systems software, applications packages, communications, special-purpose computers, which have become available since the data processing strategy was set.

10. Good data processing practice. This includes the following.

(a) Adequate **control** procedures.
(b) **Validation** of input.
(c) Use of **exception** reports and inquiry systems to minimize output.
(d) **Turn-around** documents to minimize errors and effort in input.
(e) Adoption of **standards**.

Test and communicate the solution

These are logically two steps, but in practice a great deal of the testing of the solution comes from constructing documentation, communicating it back to those involved in the system and considering their comments. Prior to this, the systems design team should return to the analysis and ensure that every feature identified has been considered in the design, by inclusion in the new system, or by exclusion with a note of the way it will be handled.

The communication of the solution will include a prime document, termed *System Definition* or *Statement of Requirements*. There may be an accompanying document with confidential material, for example the cost benefit analysis and effects on staffing. The solution is likely to be presented verbally at meetings, and amended as a result of discussion. Within the prime document, **flowcharts, decision tables** and diagrams of **information flow** will be used to show the proposed procedures.

Detailed systems design

From the previous stage, details of equipment, software, procedures and people involved will have been decided. The next stage is to turn this into a form which can be handed over to a programming team. The document produced as a result will be the **Systems Specification**. This involves:

1. Detailed **file** design, with organization and content of **records** or **data base** design.
2. Design of **forms** for input.
3. Design of all **printed reports**.
4. Display formats for **terminals**, and details of dialogue between computer and terminal user.

5. Function of each **program**, with input, output and performance constraints.
6. Schedule for the project through to live running.

Document control and change control

In the above stages documents are produced and distributed, then amended as a result of comment or changing requirements. A change control procedure is required for the proposal, consideration and authorization of changes. A document control procedure is needed, to ensure that authorized changes to documents are distributed to all those who need them, and that any document states its issue number or date of issue, so that it can readily be determined whether it is up to date.

IMPLEMENTATION

A system may run at a bureau, within the data processing department or on a computer within the user department. It may be a complete **applications package**, or a **suite** of programs developed specially for that user. The implementation phase, however, will contain the same elements.

1. Construction of **test data** and test files. These will include a typical period or batch of input, and batches with extreme and incorrect values.
2. Staff negotiation.
3. User documentation.
4. Ordering of forms and media.
5. Installation of computer equipment, terminals and communications lines.
6. Training.
7. Acceptance test.
8. Parameter setting, tailoring.
9. Data input or conversion for files.
10. Setting up error reporting and correcting procedures for hardware, software, system and communications.
11. Changeover: **pilot run**, **parallel run** or **direct change**.
12. Review.

In **parallel running**, the old and new systems are run side by side for a period and their output compared: if it is the same the old system is discontinued. This method may be impossible, for example if the old and new systems have different ways of serving customers. In this case **direct change** is necessary, which is more risky and therefore needs more thorough system testing. In either case a **pilot run** is possible, changing at one branch only and eliminating any problems before proceeding to change throughout.

Chapter 7

Program Preparation

DESIGN

Chapter 6 has taken the design to the stage of a **detailed systems specification**. The use of **applications packages** will already have been considered. If programs are to be written, the input, output and **algorithms** for processing will have been specified.

Programmers will have been involved in discussion of detailed systems design, particularly in the following areas.

1. Choice of **operating system** facilities.
2. Design of **program set**, with decisions on the use of **library sub-routines** and **utilities**.
3. Choice of **programming languages**.
4. Design of **file organization** and **data structure**.
5. Structure and **modules** of programs.

The individual programs are designed by progressively identifying tasks, deciding whether they can usefully be subdivided into further programs, modules or routines. The program design documentation accordingly should grow as tasks are designed in detail, **flowcharts** and **decision tables** being prepared in appropriate detail for coding of the program. If modules are made self-contained, the writing, testing and, later, the maintenance of the program are simplified; in large systems, in particular, the resultant economy in time and effort justifies the overhead in execution time and storage space.

Software systems are available to ease the implementation of **structured programming**. As mentioned in Chapter 6, some of them extend back into the analysis stage. Even if no formal method is in use, however, it is good practice to break the program into modules and routines and to ensure that they are clearly identified, particularly at the points which connect to other routines.

The way programs are broken into modules is one of the many aspects of the way programs are written, which should be covered in **programming standards**. An established data processing department is likely to have evolved a set of programming standards.

To assist in the separate development of routines, some language systems allow **local variables** which can be used in one module or subprogram only. The programmer of the module then knows that he has total control of that variable, even if the flow of the program has passed to another module and back. **Global variables**, which can be used anywhere throughout the program, are used to transfer information between modules.

Although many of the **algorithms** for processing will have been agreed at the system design stage, there will be many areas requiring choice by the programmer. An example would be the check that an entered date is valid: there are many published algorithms for this, and also for turning a date into a number of days from a set starting point. In this, and many other cases, the programmer can save effort and achieve a compact, complete and tested result by consulting books and periodicals, and looking at **sub-routine libraries**.

The criteria for the program design should be established. For a program to do a particular job, it takes longer to write a short program than a long one, and even longer to make the program run faster. The first area to examine is the main or most frequently repeated **processing loop** of a program. Simple changes to a program can often dramatically increase their speed.

Particular care should be taken in design when defining the condition which causes a program to proceed on from a loop to the next routine. This may, for example, use the technique of the **terminating value**, also known as a **sentinel** or **rogue value**. This is a value which cannot normally occur, such as an invoice number 999999 or a negative account number. The program **validation** should ensure that if such a value is accidentally input it is detected in the entry phase–otherwise the program may crash after a couple of years' satisfactory operation, when invoice number 999999 is reached by normal progression.

PROGRAMMING LANGUAGES

One design choice is that of programming language. An installation is likely to standardize on one or two languages for ease of program maintenance.

The origins of some **high level languages** have already been mentioned in Chapter 3. The different types of high level language are detailed below, with common examples in each case.

1. Commercial

(a) **COBOL** is the most widely used business language, designed to resemble English sentences.
(b) **RPG** (Report Program Generator) has many inbuilt functions to accelerate program writing and is used on small systems.

2. Scientific

(a) **FORTRAN** is intended to be read and written like engineering and scientific formulae.
(b) **ALGOL**, a mathematical language, has a compact and precise statement of procedures.

3. General purpose

PL/I is a combined commercial and scientific language with particular emphasis on the structuring of data.

4. Interactive

(a) **BASIC** is the most common language on microcomputers.
(b) **PASCAL** was developed to improve the structure, definition and logical flow of programs.
(c) **APL** has very powerful facilities for the manipulation of arrays and matrices.

5. Special purpose

Many languages have been developed for specific purposes such as:

(a) simulation;
(b) data base definition;
(c) machine tool control;
(d) education (e.g. **COMAL**, a structured form of **BASIC**);
(e) military real-time systems (e.g. **ADA** in the USA).

Some of these are variants of common languages, as indicated.

Separate programs in a set, or in some cases modules of one program, may be written in different languages. For example, a time-critical routine may be written in **assembler** for efficiency, or a mathematical sub-routine, already available in ALGOL, may be called from a FORTRAN program.

CODING AND COMPILATION

The programmer writes the **language statements**, from the detailed design, with **comments** incorporated. Specially formatted **coding sheets** help to keep the statements clear.

The programmer, or a colleague, can now make a **dry run** or **desk check**, taking some simple examples of data and following their path through the program. After correction of any errors found in this phase, the statements on the coding sheets are keyed by the programmer, or the data entry department, input and placed on disk storage, then entered as data to the **compiler** program. Typically this will check the **syntax** of every **statement**, that all **variable** names used have been defined, and that routines referenced have been **labelled**. The compiler will create a listing of the program, with errors found marked against statements. If there are no significant errors, the compiler will generate **object code** from the source statements and place it on disk storage. The programmer corrects the errors found by the compiler, **edits** the source code to incorporate the corrections, and the program is then compiled again. This process, shown in Figure 39, is repeated until the compilation is free of syntax errors.

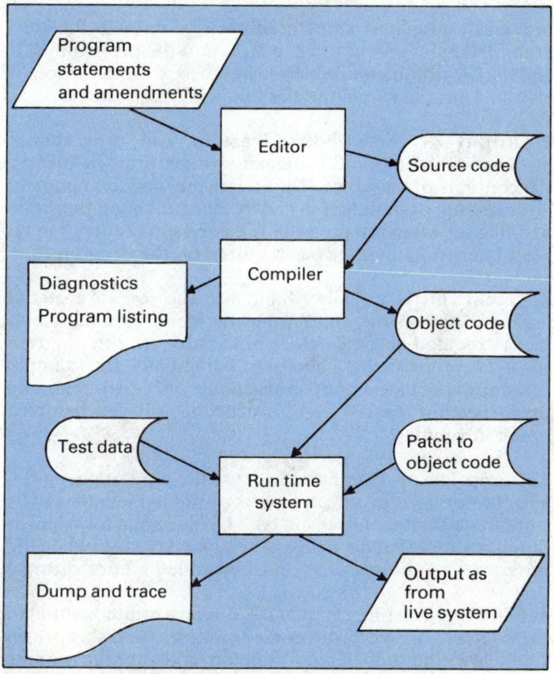

Figure 39. Program compilation and testing

Test hardware

It is often impossible or inappropriate for the programmer to use the actual equipment on which the system will run for tests. If the final system has not been delivered, the programmer may use a compatible machine and operating system elsewhere for compilation and early testing. Later a **hardware test cell** will be established, with all features of the final configuration but limited numbers of peripherals and terminals. Performance testing of the system may involve simulation of additional load, for example sending messages from disk storage as if they had originated from terminals.

In contrast, many **microprocessor** systems may have almost no input, storage and output facilities. For example, a microprocessor system used in a small toy. In these cases, a **development system** is set up containing the final microprocessor system with keyboard, display, disk and printer, in addition, to allow easy compilation and testing. When the program is finished and tested, it may be reproduced in **read-only memory** for use in live systems, to avoid the need for a device for loading the program.

TESTING AND DEBUGGING

The **object code** is loaded into memory. Sets of *test data* previously prepared and stored are run through the program. Facilities will have been built into the program itself and the environment in which it runs to ease the detection of errors. These may include the following procedures.

1. Output of intermediate results The programmer incorporates additional statements which print or display the contents of variables. The statements may be removed after testing, or their action may be dependent on the value of a flag set when the program is loaded so that they can be used later if maintenance is required on the program.

2. Trace This is a facility built into the software of the testing environment, outputting the identity of the statement executed and the values of variables as the program runs. There is usually a choice of parameters, for example printing every time a jump instruction is obeyed or retaining for inspection the last eight instructions obeyed before a break in running.

3. Dump The programmer can cause the program to pause, and the contents of selected parts of the immediate access store to be printed, usually in both hexadecimal form and in the character set of the machine. This facility, used when the program ends prematurely, is often called a **core dump**.

4. File print The programmer can obtain a printed output of the contents of selected records from files on disk storage. This allows the state of records before and after the running of the program to be compared, to ensure the correct changes have been made.

This process, of running with test data, continues until the program runs correctly. The program can then be added to other modules and run in succession with other programs in the application. At this stage the **job control language** commands, to allow the **operating system** to control the running of the application, will be written by the programmer or operations staff; these will be stored and tested with the programs. The setting of **parameters** for the particular run, and actions to take on **error conditions**, are often included in the job control language rather than in the program itself. The program can therefore now be run with fuller test data incorporating further invalid data and extreme values to test as many routes through the program as possible.

In the later stages of testing, the program should be run by someone other than the programmer who wrote it, who is likely to concentrate tests on areas which have given him trouble and may fail to see errors in other areas. Ideally the programs should be handed over to a separate validation team who will run the application using the operating instructions, as if running the programs in live operation.

One facility shown in Figure 30 is the **patch**. To use this, some additional statements in machine code are added directly to the object code rather than going through a complete compilation process. This is not a recommended procedure and should be avoided if possible. However, it is sometimes the only method available of providing a rapid solution to a problem.

Types of error

The above series of tests are intended to systematically detect errors in the programs, with the aim of providing the user with a satisfactory system. The different types of error are listed below.

1. Syntax The statement as written does not obey the rules of the language. The **compiler** or **interpreter** does not know what the programmer intended, so it flags an error. Another type of syntax error occurs if the programmer allocates a name to a variable which is a **reserved word**, i.e., one which can be used only with a special meaning. In BASIC, examples would be LIST, ERROR.

2. Code The statement is syntactically correct but is not what the programmer intended and is not in accordance with the detailed design. For example, wrong punctuation may cause a statement to transfer control prematurely. Some software assists detection of such errors, for example by taking the statements and using their logic to construct a flowchart which can then be compared with the design document. Dry running or proofreading by a colleague, or test running with simple data, will locate many errors of this type. Coding errors also arise from misunderstanding of the detailed facilities of a particular compiler and operating system and require the consultation of reference manuals for their solution.

3. Logic The detailed design of the program does not do what was intended. Counts, comparisons, initial values, calculation of record number and selection of data from a given position in a buffer are all likely to be affected. Dry running is valuable in detecting these errors and may save much testing time. This type of error is likely to put the program in an endless and useless loop when run, or may cause the program to 'fall through' to the next routine and do something totally unexpected.

4. Execution The program or module is correct when tested alone with known data but fails in conjunction with other programs. One example is data being written to a file by one program in a different format from that expected by another program. This may arise from poor communication of specification changes. The avoidance of such errors is a matter of good documentation and control. Detection is accomplished by *application testing*: this type of error is detected earlier where the programs are written from the top down, starting with the skeleton which passes data from program to program.

DOCUMENTATION AND MAINTENANCE

It should be apparent that the documentation of a program is built up as the program is designed, written and tested. It should not be left until the completion of the program. Documentation must be written at a level appropriate to its reader. In particular, *operating instructions* must be written for the user, who does not need to know how the system works, but must be told clearly how to start and proceed, and what to do if the system malfunctions.

The other technical staff, and the programmer, require detailed documentation of design to aid the future maintenance of the system. First, changes to correct the logic of the design must be incorporated into the system specification and other design documents. These should incorporate **record layouts** and lists of **variable names** with their meaning. Where **library routines** or modules from other programs have been incorporated, documentation should make clear which versions have been used and who is responsible for their maintenance. Documentation should include test data and results of test runs. If the program fails at some later date, it will then be possible to repeat the earlier tests in an attempt to isolate the fault.

Program maintenance, whether it is involved in correcting faults or changing facilities, can be a more difficult task than writing the program in the first place and, over the years, can absorb more effort.

INTERACTIVE AND INTERPRETIVE PROGRAMMING

This chapter so far has considered the program or module as part of a large system involving a team of programmers using a language system with a compiler.

A large proportion of **microcomputer** programming, whether at home, work or college, is carried out using **BASIC** and an **interpreter**. On many large data processing installations, programming is carried out using an **interactive compiler**, allowing the programmer to change and run a program from a **terminal**.

The need for documentation, modularity and planning are if anything increased for such programming. A large installation, with compilation and testing of programs in batch mode, imposes the discipline of the organization on the programmer in specifying and running his work. The individual with a microcomputer, however, can input a few lines of BASIC, run them, change them, merge in a few lines from another program and save the resultant program under a name chosen on the spur of the moment. This flexibility and immediacy is both the joy and the snare of development using an interpreter: it is easy to forget the name given to a program or file and the nature of the changes made in the last edit. It is particularly tempting to add statements in a program which branch to the middle of a useful routine elsewhere. This can make the program harder than ever to debug, and leads to bad habits which are the despair of computer science lecturers.

Here are some suggestions for avoiding these problems:

1. Keep a notebook to record program testing and development: enter at least the *names of the programs and files*.

2. Keep a folder for each program, with design notes, a list of *variable names, record and file layouts,* examples of output, *operating instructions* and source **listings** of the program.

3. Break the program into functional *modules*: any **jumps** from one module to another should be documented in an outline flowchart.

4. Add **comments** liberally to the program.

5. Include at the start of the program the *program name, date* and *version number.* If possible include this in the information displayed when the program loads, at least while the program is under development.

6. If in doubt, make a *security copy* with a name different from any used before, and put it away safely before proceeding.

7. Keep at least two previous *generations* of each program.

Chapter 8

People in Computing

ORGANIZATION OF DATA PROCESSING

There are two basic ways to structure data processing within an organization.

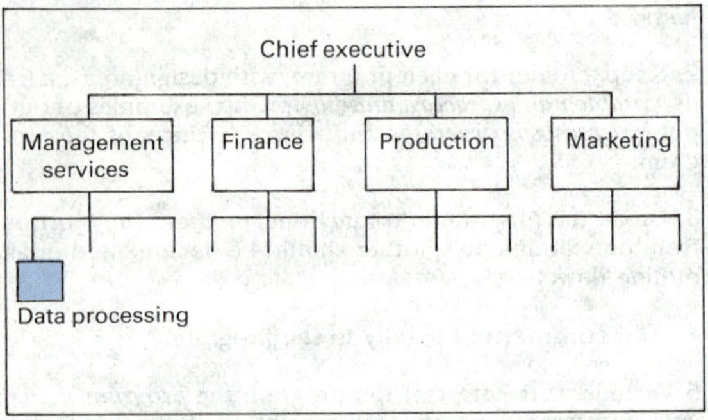

Figure 40. Central control of data processing

Figure 40 shows an example of an organization structure which can benefit from centralized control of data processing. A great deal of information must flow between the finance, production and marketing divisions. A management information services (MIS) division can satisfy the individual requirements of other divisions while still maintaining control over data formats and the equipment configuration. The goal is to facilitate smooth information flow and easy changes to systems. The MIS division must be sensitive to the changing information needs of all of the divisions and meet these needs in the best way possible.

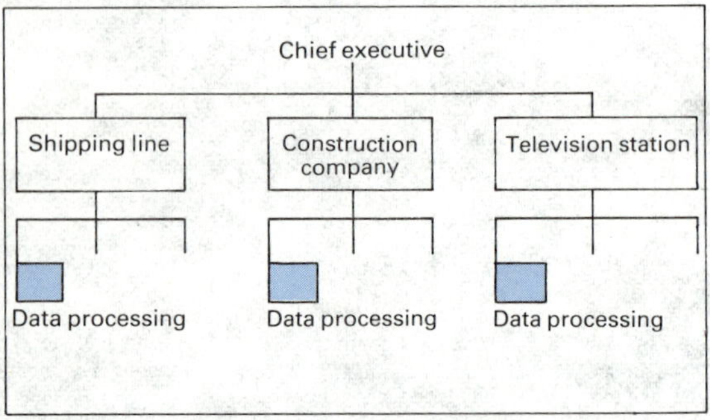

Figure 41. Data processing within functional divisions

The example of Figure 41 shows a business with separate divisions which have no need to pass information to each other. In this case, there may be no functional reason for maintaining uniformity in data, apart from ensuring that periodic financial results can be processed quickly. The divisional managers control the use of computers according to their own requirements and can implement changes more rapidly than if they were competing for resources with other divisions.

In practice the decision on centralized or distributed control is rarely clear-cut, and may appear random to the outsider not familiar with the development of the organization and the personalities within it. Sometimes there is a split between centrally controlled large computers and locally controlled small or special-purpose ones. Other organizations have a central coordination and technical team providing a service to locally controlled operations and development staff.

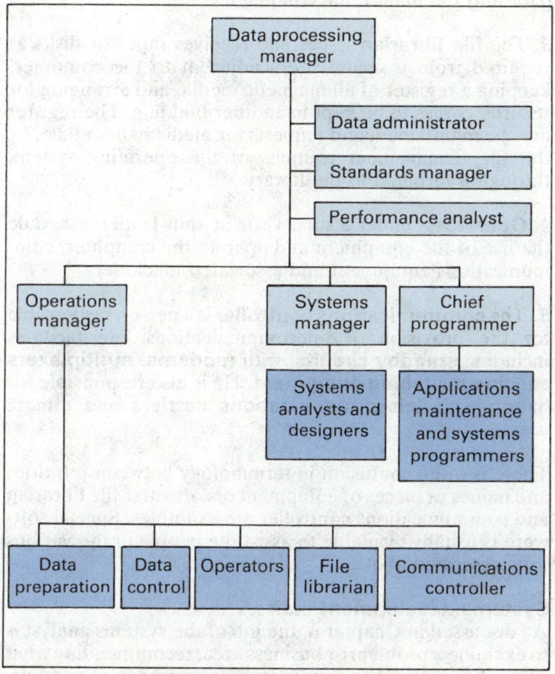

Figure 42. Structure of a MIS department

Although MIS departments may occupy different positions in the organization, there is a structure common to many of them, whether they are small or large. The various positions are described below in terms of the large batch processing systems from which this structure evolved. In smaller MIS departments a few individuals will be carrying out the functions of all these jobs. The changes in organization for varying types of data processing service are also described.

The **operations manager** is responsible for all the day-to-day running of computer systems, from collecting data to delivering results. He must supervise the following staffs.

1. Data control staff receive and record batches of documents and other data, reconciling with users errors found by validation during data preparation. They assemble completed batches into jobs for the computer, with instructions for operation, files to be used and distribution of output. This section compares control totals from processing with those of the collected batches, authorizing the release of output if correct.

2. Data preparation staff key and verify or validate the batches of documents, using card or paper tape punches, key to disk or tape machines, or terminals for direct entry of data into the mainframe computer.

3. The **file librarian** issues and receives tapes or disks as required from a secure room adjacent to the computer, keeping a register of all magnetic media, and arranging for security copies to be kept in another building. The register may be maintained, and requests for media issues made, by the file management routines of the operating system, through a terminal in the library.

4. Operators, under a supervisor or shift leader, schedule the use of the equipment and operate the computer, communications equipment and associated machinery.

5. The **communications controller** is a person responsible for the provision of telecommunications line facilities including **standby circuits**, with **modems**, **multiplexers** and **line switching equipment**. He is also responsible for liaison with **telecommunications carriers** and remote users.

There is often confusion in terminology between job titles and names of pieces of equipment or software: file librarian and communications controller are examples. Special software is usually available to assist the people in the various jobs described above.

Systems development staff

As discussed in Chapter 6, the job of the systems analyst is to examine a problem or business area, recommending what type of computer or non-computer approach is suitable. Often, a feasibility study report is written to assist top management in deciding what should be done. A project team led by a senior analyst is often established for an application once it has been authorized. There may be a split in jobs between systems analysts, who work closely with the user in establishing detailed requirements and later in implementation and training, and system designers, who work from the requirements to establish a detailed systems design in consultation with programmers. Applications tend to change over the years. This is often due to changes in the business and the law applying to it, and partly through interfaces to other computer systems being developed or because of the development of new techniques that should be incorporated in the application. There is a maintenance activity for systems staff in the development of such changes.

Programming staff

Programmers may be subdivided into three categories.

1. Applications programmers write and modify programs in accordance with specifications from the systems team. Often they work closely with users during the initial implementation of an application, the individual needs of users.

2. Maintenance programmers amend programs in operational applications, sometimes because a program has failed in operation but mainly to implement the many small changes requested by the users of the system.

3. Systems programmers are particularly concerned with the operating system and library utilities. They may write new utility programs for the installation, but are more likely to be involved in tailoring the manufacturer's operating system to run the workload efficiently, and in diagnosing reasons for software failures. Their function may be closer to the operations stream than the programming stream.

In addition to these functional sections, there will be some staff positions with responsibilities covering development and operations. These include the following.

1. The **data administrator** is responsible, as described in Chapter 5, for the data dictionary and schemas of databases.

2. The **standards manager** is responsible for maintaining standards for documentation and data interchange in particular.

3. The **performance analyst** is responsible for assessing whether the configuration can support proposed new applications or what enhancement is needed to run them, and also for monitoring the actual performance of the system and initiating changes to improve efficiency.

Variation of organization with type of processing

In a **multi-access** computing environment, the user often provides his own data control and programming, or he may use applications packages for statistics or information retrieval on files kept for him alone. Figure 43 shows the structure needed. The applications programming becomes the support of *applications packages,* and systems programmers have an increased responsibility in *systems software support.* To avoid a user, who has a problem running a program, having to refer to four separate support sections, a **user liaison** department is established to act as a single interface to users.

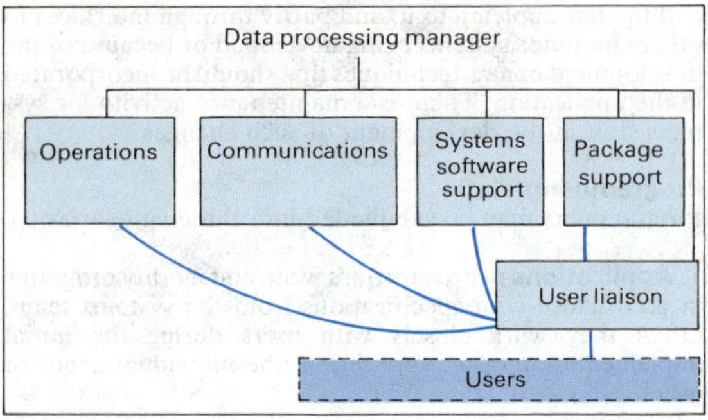

Figure 43. Organization for multi-access computing

Organization for on-line transaction processing
If one set of on-line programs for an application is to be accessed from terminals at scattered locations, the structure varies from that of Figure 42. In this case, no data preparation staff are needed, and a user liaison section is added. There will be an additional implementation section within the systems development team, including trainers to teach staff how to use the system, and implementers to go to the sites where the terminals are used. The **data control** function is no less important because data is being entered at remote terminals.

Computer time sharing service
A computer time sharing service is a commercial enterprise processing information for other concerns. The service provided may be that of running the customer's own programs, either regularly or to meet peaks and breakdowns. Alternatively, the service may provide applications packages in particular areas, either general accounting for a variety of clients or a specialist service, e.g., insurance brokers' quotations, multi-access computing or on-line information services.

Software houses
Software houses are firms developing applications programs and systems software for sale. They may develop programs to suit the requirements of a particular customer or they may produce programs which can be used by any of a variety of customers on their own computers.

SMALL SYSTEMS AND MICROCOMPUTERS

Information processing of all types is increasingly being performed by computers, often in parts of a business which have had little contact with the type of data processing department so far described. There are now large numbers of computers which have no full-time computer staff; the computer has become an adjunct of the normal duties of staff.

There are several ways in which the programs may be provided.

1. Distributed systems A concern, for example, has similar small systems at a number of locations running the same applications programs, often with communications links to a larger central computer for sending the summary results of processing. Although operations are under local control, systems development is under central control, and the central organization needed is similar to that for an on-line system.

2. Applications packages A small firm or individual department may investigate a problem and find that because it is a common problem a package is on sale which provides a solution. The firm buys the necessary software and equipment and the supplier may provide training and implementation support to put the package into operation. Word processing is an example of this.

3. Programming by user Examples are scientific users accustomed to programming using a multi-access service, and commercial users who find they can afford a microcomputer on a departmental budget.

Small business systems, data control and security
The organization described for a data processing department includes people who maintain control totals for batches of data, ensure security copies of files are kept and programs are documented to a set standard, as well as people who design and program the system, enter the data and operate the computer. Although the number of people involved in running a small system may be only one or two, with other jobs to do as well, this does not reduce the need for control, security and documentation. Indeed, one of the safeguards against fraud in a computer installation is the division of responsibility to ensure that no one person can design, control and operate a system; in a small department special control measures may be needed to obtain equivalent safeguards.

The highest risk is of loss of data or programs through carelessness or equipment failure. The most important part of a security routine is to make copies of files and programs regularly. This applies just as much to a student project as to the taxation records of the country.

Making copies of files away from the computer site is an essential safeguard against fire. Even if a firm is insured against loss of business through fire, the records in the files are the very ones required to prove to the insurers that the business existed.

The degree of data control required for protection against fraud is a commercial decision. Control costs money, but much of the information processed represents money, and a small system will rarely have the protection from unauthorized access that a large computer installation has.

DEVELOPMENT INTERACTIONS

Figure 44 shows the changing interactions in a system as it progresses: the organization is shown for a data processing manager and user working within a division of a business.

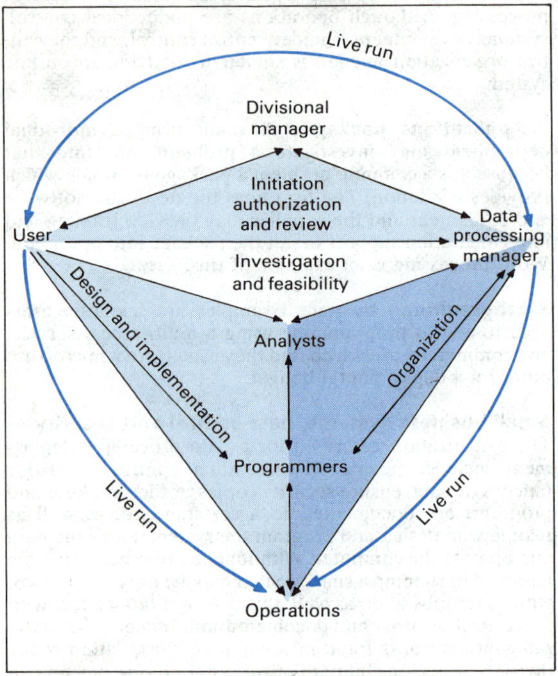

Figure 44. Interactions in processing and development

1. Initiation and authorization The stimulus for the development of a new system may come from top management, from a user or from the data processing department. It may result from outside pressure on the business from suppliers, competitors or from those to whom it provides information. Authorization of new computer systems is often at top management level. This phase alternates with the next phase, described below, until the project is authorized or dropped.

2. Investigation and feasibility This phase is primarily the job of the systems analyst, working with the user and reporting to the data processing manager. An initial feasibility report is followed by a full statement of requirements.

3. Design and implementation The systems analysts produce a detailed design in consultation with programmers, who then write the programs. These are run for testing singly and then together by operations staff, with reports and display formats being evaluated by the user. The next stages in this phase are acceptance testing, followed by pilot or parallel running.

4. Live running After implementation, the system continues with the user feeding data to the system, and operations providing results back to the user. The data processing manager discusses the smooth running of the system with both.

5. Review When the system is live it is reviewed: technically, to assess its performance and use of computer resources; functionally, to ensure it does what the user wants; and financially, to compare the costs and benefits with those predicted.

Later changes to the system involve a repeat of these phases on a smaller scale.

PLANNING

One problem for the data processing manager and the users is that the time needed to develop a new computer system may be similar to the time for which the business objectives remain unaltered, and that the time taken to obtain agreement and authorization eats into the available development time. The solution to this, easier to recommend than to implement, is to maintain a strategic data processing plan for the next five years. This should contain, in particular, the major elements of policy: centralization or distributed control, use of database techniques and use of communications networks. The plan will contain in outline the applications expected to be implemented, and will allow long-term scheduling of resources of men and machines. As specific projects are authorized the plan is updated to accommodate them.

From the point of view of the data processing department, the major features of the plan for an individual project are the times at which it is necessary to allocate systems analysts, programmers, computer time for testing, operators for live running, and to obtain computers, lines and terminals. Delays in availability or prolongation of stages delay other stages and other projects, but do not drastically alter the department. However, the user department must plan for a change in its method of working when the new system is introduced. This may involve moving existing staff to other work, training staff to cope with new working methods, and moving people permanently from one location to another. The effect of delay can be far more disruptive in the user department than in the data processing department, as these plans may have to be reversed.

It is advisable to prepare and maintain a network or activity chart, showing the actions and resources needed by the project and their interrelationship. Regular reporting, as milestones in the plan are passed, allows management to monitor progress and recover any time lost. The very fact of having to report progress against a detailed plan has a substantial influence in maintaining schedules. Management should insist that deadlines as set in the plan are actually met.

AUDIT

The crucial phase in the audit of a computer-based accounting system comes before the system is run, i.e., during the systems design and systems testing phases. At the design stage the auditor can ensure that adequate controls are included. At the testing phase he can satisfy himself that test data is correctly processed and invalid data is rejected and reported. He can also ensure that test data is retained for use in later operational audits.

Once the system is operational it is likely to be far more difficult to introduce facilites for the auditor. In a batch system, he can follow an input batch through the system, checking output against source documents. In a real time system there may be no source documents to check. However, it should be possible to arrange for all input from one terminal to be extracted from transaction logs, and to follow through the processing of this input.

It is clear that, where computer systems are involved, the auditor requires a substantial knowledge of data processing to do his job effectively. Various file processing packages are available to assist auditors in the examination of records.

Chapter 9

Applications

PACKAGE SOFTWARE

Many concerns have similar information processing requirements to such an extent that computer manufacturers and software houses are able to write **applications packages** which can be used by many different companies.

This has the following advantages for the user.

1. The system can be implemented quickly.

2. The expense of programming is limited to the purchase of the package and fees for updating.

3. The package will have been tested and run elsewhere, so it can be expected to run with little trouble.

4. The early use of a good package, satisfying a large proportion of stated requirements, may help to clarify residual requirements.

In specifying a package, analysts have to identify the procedures common to many concerns, the options likely to be required and the ways in which output needs to be tailored to the specific user. The following elements form the essence of many business packages.

1. A set of logical processing modules is used, which the user can select, often by choice, from a menu of alternatives.

2. A set of files is used, with common organization but in which the user can select the number of occurrences of each type of data, up to a maximum.

3. Output formats are given in which the user can 'fill in the blanks' in the headings while setting up the system.

4. Parameters are used to set constants into the program for a particular run.

There are, however, several limitations of the package approach.

1. The package has to allow for many options: the programs may occupy more memory and run more slowly than if specially written.

2. The procedures are pre-set: in order to use the package, a concern may have to change its clerical procedures to suit the package.

3. In catering for a wide range of possibilities, output may contain extraneous, unwanted and even meaningless information.

4. The use of packages may make the integration of procedures across an organization more difficult.

Some packages are used on an *ad hoc* basis, while others become part of the routine information flow. An example of each type is given below, with samples of the choices and ranges of data which might be found in commercial packages.

A statistical package (Least squares fit of data with time trend)

1. Input number of observations (up to 200).
2. Input time units (day, week, month, year).
3. Input data.
4. Correct wrong input.
5. Save data on disk.
6. Goodness of fit of data to eight different function types (e.g. linear, exponential) is output.
7. For projection of trend, choose:

(a) final date;
(b) table or graph;
(c) labels for columns or axes.

A hotel management package

1. Setting up

(a) Choose room description set, e.g., S = Single, D = Double.
(b) Input sales point names, e.g., 1 = Penguin Bar, 2 = Hungry Horse Restaurant.
(c) Input discount rates, e.g., 0 (Default option) = 0%, 1 = 10%, etc.
(d) Tax rates and accounting periods are similarly input.

2. Initial data entry

(a) Input number and description of each room.
(b) Input bookings for 12 months.
(c) Output bookings chart and compare with diary, making corrections as necessary.
(d) Take security copies of files.

3. Daily operations

(a) Choose facility, e.g., inquiry.
(b) Input start date/room type/number of nights.
(c) Choose:
0 Terminate.
1 Room available: go to booking procedure.
2 Display available rooms.
3 Display all rooms.

The statistical package has no initial setting up and each run is independent. The hotel package, however, requires a substantial phase to tailor it to the requirements of the hotel and a large amount of input data to change from the existing manual system.

The period of changeover from a manual system to an applications package requires as much attention as would be given to specially written programs. In the above example, bookings would be recorded manually for a period, in parallel to entry into the computer package.

Package choice

The following steps are required in choosing a package.

1. Identify requirements The physical capacities and procedural facilities of available packages need to be compared and matched to the requirements.

2. Assess vendor It is advisable to check how long the package has been in use and to visit other users. The availability of future maintenance and support needs to be assessed.

3. Assess implications If the package were to be used, what would be the resultant operation? Changes to procedures, ways in which ancillary computer operations may be affected and the requirements of the auditors all need to be considered.

Documentation

Documentation is important for any computer system. For a package it is crucial: in most cases it is the only link with the programmers and system designers. The documentation is used to answer the following questions.

1. Will it do the required job?
2. How do I set the package to suit the equipment and organization?
3. How do I prepare the data?
4. How do I secure the data and files?
5. How do I deal with run time options, parameters and errors?

TYPES OF APPLICATION

As businesses grow in complexity and computers extend to more facets of processing of information for business, government and the public, so the applications grow in scope and variety, making it difficult to place them in watertight categories. One method of subdividing the types of processing is given below.

1. Administration: repetitive; large data volumes.
2. Information movement: lists; text; office automation; selection from large data stores.
3. Control: frequent and rapid processing; matching and reservation.
4. Planning: small volumes; extensive processing; optimization.

Processing can also be subdivided according to the time-scale of the response.

1. Batch processing The response occurs at the end of a period during which transactions are grouped.
2. Transaction processing This is real time, on-line, with immediate response.

Although this time-scale split has far-reaching effects on the computer systems and the way people interact with them, it is the surrounding operation rather than the manipulation of the information which is changed.

Selected applications will now be reviewed by broad grouping of concern.

COMMERCIAL BUSINESS

The administration of commerce occupies more computer systems than all other applications. In this category are the bread and butter of computing: payroll; accounting for sales and purchases; customer accounting for banks and other institutions which transfer, lend and borrow money. Insurance companies, for renewals, and public utilities, for billing, are concerns making heavy use of computers in this way. Although, in many cases, these applications have been mechanized for fifty years and computerized for twenty, their development is by no means static. Sales accounting is extending to the retailer, with **point of sale** systems including **bar code readers** at cash registers. Credit cards have extended the cashless transfer of funds; **magnetic strips** on the cards and **terminals** on-line allow instant credit checking and account debiting.

The next level of application adds a control element within the day-to-day operation. An **inventory control** system may not only record movements but compare levels with set minima and issue orders for replenishment; it may also itself set stockholding levels by analysis of usage including both overall trends and seasonal variations. The economic ordering quantity and lead time for supply can be incorporated.

Production control systems link information on orders, production machines and material to be processed, scheduling movements and processes to achieve time and money requirements. These systems have changed progressively from end-of-day reporting to real time control systems. As computing power becomes less expensive, the real-time control of interacting operations is becoming more common.

This leads to the application of **automation** of processes, where the computer is not only supplying a schedule but directly controlling the settings of machines and handling of materials. Two approaches to automation co-exist. In one, a special-purpose machine has sensors and remotely controlled actuators added, and linked to a **process control com-**

puter. The other approach is to build **robots**, computer-controlled manipulators, which can be programmed to perform a series of handling operations and, with change of program and fittings, can perform a totally different series. The flexibility of control of robots encourages **artificial intelligence** and **heuristic** techniques, in which the robot may learn its movements from a human operator, and then proceed to learn the effects of variations to allow correction and improvement of the quality of output.

In **distribution**, firms with a variety of factories, warehouses and vehicles have the complex problem of choosing the most economic pattern of supply. These problems can be solved by various mathematical programming techniques. For practically any realistic problem of this type, a computer is required for solution, due to the large number of variables and volume of calculation required. The reader is referred to the book *Computer Applications* in this series, which contains a number of examples of these problems.

As an example of mathematical programming, specifically linear programming, consider an ice cream manufacturing company with two factories (A, B) and three cold stores (X, Y, Z). Figure 45 shows the capacity of manufacture at each source, the sales demand in the area served by each cold store, and, for each combination, the unit cost of manufacture and distribution combined.

	Coldstore			
	X	Y	Z	
Factory A	Cost 38 AX	Cost 42 AY	Cost 40 AZ	Capacity 10 000
Factory B	Cost 40 BX	Cost 39 BY	Cost 41 BZ	Capacity 20 000
	Demand 6000	Demand 10 000	Demand 13 000	Total 30 000 / Total 29 000

Figure 45. Matrix for a linear programming solution

The constraints are:

$ax + ay + az$ is less than or equal to 10 000.
$bx + by + bz$ is less than or equal to 20 000.
$ax + bx = 6000$, $ay + by = 10\,000$, $az + bz = 13\,000$.

The requirement is to minimize cost, given by:

$$\text{Cost} = 38ax + 42ay + 40az + 40bx + 39by + 41bz.$$

The method is to choose one solution satisfying the constraints, evaluate the cost and then move one step to another solution. If cost is the same or improved, further changes are made, moving from this solution or from the better previous one. This proceeds until changes give no further improvement and thus the optimum has been attained.

This method has very wide application in transportation and is also used in optimizing the blending of animal foods and oil refinery feedstock.

In management planning, computer applications assist business decisions. An application which has increased rapidly with the availability of microcomputer packages is **financial forecasting**, where the manager can input a spreadsheet of figures and try the effect of variations, asking 'What if?' questions. These packages allow the planner to quickly model a situation and evaluate alternatives, producing both reports and charts as output.

Another important application is project management using either **critical path analysis** or **PERT** (Project Evaluation and Review Technique). These techniques are used for assessing and controlling the duration, resource requirement and cost of projects (see *Production* in this series).

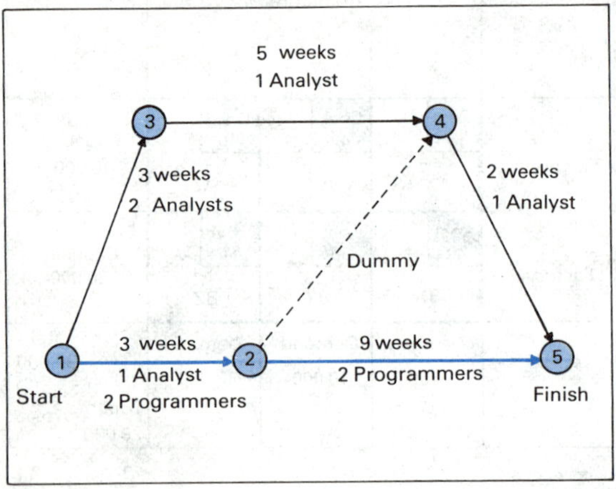

Figure 46. A PERT network

In this technique, for each activity of a project, the analyst first assesses:

1. The expected duration of the activity, using normal resources;

2. The other events which must be completed before the activity can start.

Working forward through the events reveals the earliest completion date for each event. Working backward from the end then gives the latest possible completion date for each event which does not affect the total duration of the project. If these are the same, the event is on the **critical path**. For an event on another path, the difference is known as the **float**, which applies to the complete path not just a single activity. In Figure 46, path 1–3–4–5 has two weeks' float and path 1–2–5 is the critical path. Activity 4–5 cannot commence until event 2 is complete, so a **dummy activity** 2–4, with no duration or resource requirement, is included in the chart to show this constraint.

Resource analysis may then determine the feasibility of the plan. In the example given, if only two programmers and two analysts are available, activity 1–3 cannot commence until event 2 is achieved, but this delays completion. **Cost analysis** can then be applied to various alternatives, such as overtime working or employment of temporary staff, to decide how and whether to apply resources to finish on time.

This technique allows reviews of progress to concentrate on events on the critical path, and on other events on which slippage is predicted which might put them onto the critical path.

Office automation A group of applications which mainly involve the movement and manipulation of written and spoken text are increasing in importance. **Word processing** allows text to be typed, with the inclusion of standard paragraphs, to be stored, corrected and printed in a desired format. **Electronic mail** allows such text to be sent to remote locations and stored, displayed or printed there. Facsimile transmission also allows pictures and graphs to be sent from one location to another using telephone lines. Computer-controlled telephone exchanges and switchboards allow calls to be automatically dialed, grouped and diverted. Currently, there are many commercial information services available in the United States which give users access to nationwide electronic mail, news and stock market data.

GOVERNMENT AND PUBLIC ADMINISTRATION

Public organizations have sections which are run in the same way and have the same problems as commercial business, so the applications described above are often useful. Other applications are particular to the public sector.

In the administrative use of computers, public sector applications are characterized by *very large data volumes,* so large that exceptions which would occur rarely and be handled manually in business occur with such frequency that they require computer processing. Therefore, both the files and the programs used have to be large and complex. In licenses and taxes on income, vehicles and property, and in the various census counting and statistical activities, volumes are approximately one per person or household. The *social* and *privacy* implications of these all-embracing files are discussed in Chapter 10.

Other applications, such as hospital admissions, issues of books from libraries and student records in schools, are of more obvious benefit to the individual.

The public sector has particular control applications. **Air traffic control** computers allow more airliners to use an airport than could be handled by men alone. **Road traffic control** across the whole city involves decisions on thousands of relationships of traffic signals: without computer aid the pattern of control has to be pre-set, with no way of allowing for day-to-day variations. **Command and control** systems for emergency services can identify the nearest police vehicle to an incident, track the response, and provide information on stolen cars, actions to deal with hazardous chemicals and beds available at hospitals.

The **education** sector uses computers for administration and information, as well as for teaching: computer-aided instruction is a growing field much influenced by the ready availability of microcomputers.

Military applications of computers include large-scale provisioning, command and control on the battlefield, control systems built into warplanes and missiles. There are many project management applications. Much of the early development of PERT was for the construction of nuclear submarines. **Simulation** techniques are used for **war games**, allowing the result of a battle using certain weapon systems to be assessed in advance. Computers are extensively used in communications, in the encoding of messages for security and in the breaking of codes.

In **weather forecasting** the equations governing the motion of air and the condensation of water are known, so in theory a computer **model** of the atmosphere could be constructed. In practice, the complexity and required speed are still beyond the scope of current computers. Approximations are used for short-range forecasts, while long-range forecasting uses computers to find periods with a similar pattern of weather, using past records. The collection of data from land stations and satellites itself makes heavy use of computers.

SCIENCE AND DESIGN

In design, the engineer uses the ability of the computer to hold the rules of behavior and interaction of materials, and the ability – which has resulted from complex programming – to provide two-dimensional pictures from any direction of three-dimensional objects. This allows the designer of a vehicle or bridge to piece together his design from components, to view the result and to assess the effect of load, wind and other factors. **Computer-aided design** has been used in many applications: for civil engineering, where complex stress calculations are needed over many components; on vehicles, where appearance and performance must proceed together in the design; on airplanes, where stress, weight and aerodynamics must be calculated; in the layout of printed circuit boards and integrated circuits, where the sheer number of lines and interconnections would now take a draftsman longer to produce than the time which would elapse before the design became obsolete!

Scientific literature is published at an increasing rate. The researcher, trying to find references to particular combinations of effects, could spend a great deal of time searching literature and abstracts for references, without being confident that the search was complete. By inputting **keywords** describing each effect to a computerized **information retrieval** service, references to all scientific papers with that particular combination can be obtained quickly. If the number found is large, criteria can be further narrowed or the most recent references can be selected.

Much of science involves the analysis of results to extract the underlying structure, and computers can handle the complex and numerous calculations involved. An example is the analysis of X-ray diffraction patterns, from which crystals with thousands of atoms can be analyzed by computer whereas, before, the manual analysis of tens of atoms was very difficult. Another example is the analysis of spectral observations from satellites, where the results are analyzed together with the orbit of the satellite, resulting in geological maps of previously unexplored areas, for example.

COMPUTERS IN THE PROFESSIONS

Professions such as law and medicine use computers for accounting and information retrieval as well as for the other applications mentioned above. A growing field of particular relevance to the professions is that of **expert systems**. In medicine this takes the form of computer-aided diagnosis. A patient's symptoms are entered into the computer, together with the results of any tests and answers obtained in a dialogue between the computer and the patient, using a terminal. From textbooks, and from the knowledge of leading experts in particular fields, combinations of symptoms pointing to particular diseases are progressively entered into the computer, which can then give a list of possible diagnoses, with the probabilities for each, and can propose tests to narrow the possibilities. This type of system can use learning techniques to improve its performance, by adding to its store new diagnoses and combinations as they are discovered. This approach is possible in many fields of expertise; the analysis and programming are a more involved and longer procedure than for a business system and produce possibilities rather than decisions. The availability of such a system to a young doctor allows the accumulated experience of a number of consultants to bear on his problem, and therefore allows the young doctor to work at a higher level of expertise than before.

BENEFITS OF COMPUTER SYSTEMS

The benefits of a computer system have to be related to the aims of the enterprise and to the contribution of the system to those aims. A cost comparison is the most direct and convincing assessment of the benefit of a system. Cost comparisons can be made according to the following guidelines.

1. Cost of present system.
2. Cost of proposed computer system – capital, staff and running costs.
3. Direct cost changes, e.g., staff redeployed, inventory-holding reduced.
4. Indirect and intangible changes, e.g., better customer service.
5. Effect on old and new systems of projected future volumes.
6. Commonality – effect on allied systems.

In a commercial enterprise, the assessment of intangible benefits in this type of analysis must relate to realizable flows of money. Similar analysis in a non-commercial concern may be more hypothetical, putting a value on the relief of suffering or the prestige of winning races.

Some systems may provide benefit by the quantification of risk; for a festival, the chance of rain is an insurable risk, and knowledge from weather forecasting of the probability of rain is worth money both to the organizer and to the insurance company.

There are now some computer applications which, in the present state of technology, can only be performed by digital electronic computers–space mission control is an example. These are applications requiring large numbers of calculations in a limited time, arriving at a result about one item, e.g., nuclear reactor, oil refinery, crystal structure. Other large-scale applications such as government licensing operations, banks and electric power companies have evolved a structure over the years which is now totally dependent on the use of computers. In these cases the benefit of a computer system cannot be considered in isolation, although the costs and facilities of different computer systems for that application can be compared.

As discussed in the next chapter, the social effects of computer systems are of increasing concern. The balance of social benefits must be considered together with the balance of cost benefit in assessing the impact of a system on an organization and its members.

Chapter 10

Social Effects

This chapter considers the effects that the spread of computers have on individuals – their jobs, their homes, organizations in which they work, and their society and environment. It also considers some aims for the future of computing.

SECURITY AND PRIVACY

The most debated aspect of the way computers affect the lives of everyday people is that of privacy and security. Information about individuals has been collected by government departments and commercial enterprises for thousands of years. Instead of collecting this on pieces of paper and storing it in filing cabinets in their own offices, organizations can now keep information in magnetic form at a computer center and retrieve data through terminals.

This can create problems for the individual through ease of communication, access, collation and searching, and through incorrect data being used.

The data in question may be a record of a person's employment, school career, health, credit rating, encounters with police and civil law suits. Dissemination of information on any of these areas may affect the individual's future. In making access available for the rightful owners or users of the data, particularly through terminals and communications lines, the computer system may also make access easy for unauthorized users. There is a duty, which has been made a legal responsibility in some countries, to build safeguards into a system to limit unauthorized access. Such measures include **passwords** to enter from terminals, physical locks on terminals, insertion of **punched** or **magnetically encoded cards** into terminals to gain access, and rigid restrictions on entry to computer rooms.

However, authorized access is far more of a problem than unauthorized access. If there are no restrictions on the way an organization is allowed to show or sell data, the individual can find his private life laid bare to the world. The facts recorded may be half-truths, or may even apply to a different person. In the field of information about credit standing, in particular, some countries have introduced laws allowing a record to be seen and corrected by the individual to whom it refers.

The culmination of these fears felt by many individuals is that government will succeed in collating all the information contained in the multiplicity of files about individuals and use this for control purposes. This has been prevented more by the size of the files and differences in organization and record keying within them than by any lack of will on the part of government departments. Indeed, some very large collated files about groups of individuals have already been formed.

The organization as well as the individual is at risk from invasions of the security and privacy of information held in computers. Information about a company's past performance, present products and future plans may all be held in its computers, and are all worth money to competitors or stock market gamblers. Large amounts of money may be involved, and the criminal may be prepared to go to a lot of trouble to steal information, bribing operators or maintenance engineers, tapping wires to copy messages or installing a terminal to masquerade as a genuine user. In many cases little equipment is needed: skilled infiltrators may gain access by exploring the system from a terminal until a path in is discovered.

Information may not only be copied but changed or destroyed, using the power of the computer system and the increase in cashless money transactions to divert funds. One example is the setting up of a bogus supplier and authorizing payments to it. Another is the application of small increases to service charges for numerous customers and diversion of the surplus to an account which is later cleared. Protection against abuse is by vigilance, audit, control, division of responsibility and reduction of opportunity.

EFFECTS ON ORGANIZATIONAL STRUCTURE

The economy of scale of large computers has led to centralization of data processing, which has contributed in many organizations to more control throughout. This leads to bureaucratic rules being imposed from the center, resulting in very little autonomy for the manager of an outlying office or department. With the availability of cheap microprocessors, which can be linked to central mainframes, this trend can be reversed. The data originating in a local office can be processed in the office, with a summary only being sent to the head office. The departmental manager can regain responsibility for his own information and results. Furthermore, there is less reason for head office functions to be concentrated in one place: these can be distributed around the country or even around the world, if appropriate.

It is much easier to purchase and implement a microprocessor system in one office than to develop a large integrated system across an organization, resulting in conflicts between central management services departments and individual users. The former see it as their duty to standardize and coordinate the holding and processing of data, so that the whole concern can be run as a coherent whole and react uniformly to future change. There is also an element of self-interest: when a department has obtained the job of processing data for the whole organization, it does not want to lose it. The individual departmental manager wants quick implementation of systems to suit his local needs, since he is being assessed on the results he obtains in the current year.

This can lead to a proliferation of incompatible systems distributed around the organization. Some organizations are attempting to steer a middle course by allowing individual departments to purchase only particular makes of microcomputer, thus maintaining substantial compatibility while giving independence.

One effect of the concentration of data processing has been the ability of a few computer operators to go on strike and by so doing bring the whole money collection mechanism of an organization virtually to a halt. Thus, one aspect of systems which should be reviewed, along with their benefits, is the increased risk from industrial disputes, terrorist action, accidents and theft.

In some cases computer systems which change the work structure have led to major industrial disputes. Problems arise particularly where many different unions are involved, and the change would involve redistribution of work between them. In other cases, staff participation in planning has led to computer systems which enhance the jobs of those involved. Either way, any system which changes the structure of a concern needs early consultation, and careful consideration of the balance of social benefits as well as cost benefits.

The convergence of communications and data processing, together with relaxations in the monopolies of national telecommunications authorities, has led computer service companies to set up as communications carriers, and vice versa. This trend is further complicated by the use of domestic television receivers as terminals, which draws broadcasting and cable TV companies into the same fields.

EMPLOYMENT

The increasing use of computers has produced employment opportunities in the design, production, distribution, operation and maintenance of computer systems and their applications software. This is accompanied by losses and changes in jobs affected by the use of computers. A supervisor may benefit when a computer takes over his tedious desk work, leaving him to concentrate on direct interaction with his staff, but this is also likely to reduce the number of supervisors needed. If an inspection process is automated so that the tolerances of a component are checked by a microprocessor, the job content of quality control staff will change, requiring them to have either the higher skills of specifying tests and evaluating results, or the lower skills of machine minding. Previous technological advances have brought changes in employment, but the rate of change induced by computers is considerably higher. Staff will have to be retrained for different jobs several times in their working lives.

Another area in which computers affect individuals is that, with the spread of communications and microcomputers to more and more types of information processing, the numbers of people who themselves operate computers or terminals as part of their jobs increases. This transition can be very difficult and even lead to stress and illness, particularly for older people not accustomed to thinking in the ways of the computer. However, many jobs are being simplified by the use of computers. In many cases, workers in offices, manipulating words and numbers, exercise skill and judgment as before, but now have the help of computers with the more tedious tasks of entering figures on sheets, adding and checking, and summarizing.

Office automation has concentrated first on document production, as giving the earliest cost benefits and not requiring standardization of communication. The biggest changes in the office, however, will come from the use of processing, communications, and information services by professional and managerial staff, making them more productive and more effective. Today, the decreasing cost of microprocessor based computer systems, which have the ability to be linked together into **local area networks**, is rapidly accelerating the move toward office automation.

Information technology can be used in the office to enrich jobs. Where in the past application of Organization and Work Methods techniques led to fragmentation of clerical procedures, to allow specialization and increase efficiency, the use of electronic aids can help to reassemble the component parts of the job and place responsibility for the whole job back with the individual. When procedures no longer depend on documents being manually processed and handed on quickly to the next person in the chain, flexible working hours and arrangements for staff to work from home are made easier.

Jobs not only change – they disappear. In many organizations, over the last 20 years, the effects of large central computers have been to allow slowly increasing numbers of staff to deal with rapidly increasing volumes of business and flows of information. With world recession, these changes in industry have become more apparent. The changes are not only those associated with computing: there are changes from heavy to light industry and from manufacturing to service industry. To remain competitive, industry has to use technology to increase productivity: the spread of automation and robots is an obvious manifestation of this. Mechanical and electromechanical products are being replaced by microelectronics. For example, the Swiss watch industry has substantially declined as a result of the introduction of digital watches made in other countries.

ENVIRONMENT

Computer systems affect many of the interactions between the individual and the society in which he lives. If computers increase productivity and reduce costs of manufacture, the prices of goods in the shops can fall or dividends from shares can rise. If production schedules, quality, distribution and inventory holdings are better controlled, then there is less likelihood of having to wait for supplies or of returning faulty goods. Credit cards and Electronic Funds Transfer Systems (EFTS) reduce the amount of cash that needs to be carried, and the time spent waiting in banks. Doctors' handwriting on prescriptions is notoriously bad: if the dose to be taken is automatically checked against standards when a prescription is made up and labelled, then added protection against misunderstanding is afforded. The safety of air travel is also improved: landings can be made automatically in poor visibility and collisions can be averted.

However, as computer systems come to be increasingly relied upon they acquire an apparent immutable power. Administration systems in particular have become so complex that no one programmer understands or can reconstruct the logic behind them. In this they resemble taxation: governments pass laws, accountants find and exploit loopholes, governments pass more laws to plug the gaps in the old ones, and no one dares overhaul the structure for fear of the chaos that might result. Computer systems evolve in the same way, with users at terminals finding other ways of achieving prohibited transactions, and programmers patching in routines to catch them. In these systems computers therefore tend to preserve the status quo, rather than being agents of change. Interacting with these systems, it is easy to suffer from the delusion that the computer is generating decisions, when in fact these follow from the actions of the succession of analysts and programmers who have designed and maintained the system, and the users who have specified the requirements.

HOME COMPUTING

In a few years there will be as many computers in the home as there are electric motors now. Many of them will be integral parts of other products, not recognizable as computers. Cameras, central heating, locks, burglar alarms, sound systems, telephones, television sets, washing machines and ovens are but a few items which will be controlled by individual computers.

The disabled in particular can benefit. Computer input and output can be in a form convenient for the individual. Someone with no control over their hands can communicate, and control, by sucking and blowing. For the blind, machines have been developed which can read aloud by optical recognition from typescript.

Home computers use computer-aided learning for education, data bases for holding details of collections for hobbies and accounting packages for bank balances. There are, however, two factors which probably account for most home computing. One is that many people enjoy the intellectual stimulus of programming, to the extent that some become 'code junkies' living only for the thrill of the next error message. The other, initially to the great surprise of the microcomputer manufacturers, is the vast popularity of all manner of games played with computers.

FUTURE AIMS OF COMPUTING

Computing equipment has become progressively faster while processing and storage equipment have also become progressively cheaper. It has been estimated that the microprocessor-based business computers available today have the power of the mainframe computers available in the late 1950s. This reduction in cost has resulted in the software of computer systems becoming an increasing proportion of the total cost. One approach to this problem is the development of increasingly sophisticated applications packages, allowing the user to select from tested modules those which best suit his problem, building the system by answering questions from the package generator.

Current computers have been developed primarily for numerical calculation. The processing of text, speech and pictures requires equipment to be used in ways for which it was not designed. The flexibility of logic allows this to be done, but the programming involved becomes extremely complex and the speed of processing is low. Increasingly, as computers spread into more fields of information processing, input and output as sound and pictures will be needed.

Computer scientists throughout the world have been considering future developments in computing. In 1979 the Japanese government set up a committee to review world computing and consider its future. As a result a collaborative development project has been started, and in 1981 the aims and possible methods of achieving them were discussed at an international symposium.

Because Japan has set up a formal project to consider the aims of computing for the 1990s, and how they might be implemented, much of the discussion of the long-term future of computing has stemmed from the conferences and reports on the Japanese **fifth generation** of computers.

The goals of the fifth generation project, as summarized by Cahill in *Computer Weekly*, July 15, 1982, are given below.

Strategic problems the technology is expected to solve

1. To increase productivity in low-productivity areas, such as agriculture, fishing, distribution and the public services.

2. To help Japan meet international competition and at the same time enable Japan to make a significant contribution to international cooperation.

3. To assist in saving energy.

Functional requirements for the technology

1. A man-machine interface at the input-output level, which would operate on spoken language, graphics, images and documents.

2. The conversion of stored information into practical use.

3. The ability to perform inferential logic operation, as well as process data conventionally.

4. To eliminate, from an end user point of view, the use of most current programming languages.

Further Reading

Burch, J.G. Jr., Stratter, F.R., and Grudnitski, G., *Information Systems: Theory and Practice* (John Wiley and Sons, 1983)

Newmann, N. and S., *Principles of Information Systems for Managements* (Wm. C. Brown Co.)

Stair, R.M., Jr., *Principles of Data Processing: Concepts, Applications and Cases* (Richard D. Irwin, Inc., 1981)

Taggert, W.M., Jr., *Information Systems: An Introduction to Computers in Organizations* (Allyn and Bacon, Inc., 1980)

Glossary

Accumulator A storage circuit in the arithmetic and logic unit holding the data resulting from an instruction.
Ada A programming language for military applications, named after **Ada** Countess Lovelace, the first programmer.
Address Identification of the location of data in store, or of a peripheral device.
ALGOL A mathematical programming language.
Algorithm A definition of a problem solution in a finite number of steps.
Analog Data that are held and manipulated as continuously variable physical quantities; hence analog computer (also spelled *analogue*).
APL (A Programming Language) Particularly suited for interactive, mathematical applications.
Arithmetic and logic unit The part of a central processor containing the electronic circuits for the manipulation of data.
Array An arrangement of items of data such that the position of an item is given by a set of subscripts, one for each dimension of the array.
ASCII A standard 8-bit code for character representation.
Assembler A program taking mnemonic statements written by the programmer in assembly language, and converting each statement to a machine code instruction.
Bar code A pattern of lines printed on the packaging of goods in retail shops, encoding the product identity to allow optical reading at the checkout.
BASIC An interactive high level programming language.
Batch processing Performed when data for input are accumulated for a period before processing and providing results.
Batch total A total of the values in the same field in all records of a batch, accumulated outside the computer and later checked within the computer as a control.
BCD (Binary Coded Decimal) A code in which decimal digits are represented by patterns of 4 bits.
Binary Numbering system to the base 2.
Bit (from BInary digiT) One of the two digits used in the binary system. It is the smallest unit of information.
Block Several records of data, not necessarily related, which are stored or moved as one unit.
Boolean algebra A set of rules of logical combinations of variables which stand for statements that can only be true or false.
Branch A change in program sequence (*see* Jump).
Bug An error in a program.
Bus An equipment inter-connection in which a number of different devices are connected to one set of signal lines from a processor.
Byte A group of bits, usually 8, considered as a unit.
Central processor The part of a computer which controls the other parts and performs operations on data in accordance with the stored program. It includes the arithmetic

and logic unit, the control unit and the memory.

Channel An equipment inter-connection from a processor such that each device has a separate set of signal lines.

Check digit A digit added to a reference number, to aid detection of errors in data collection and processing. The check digit has a set relationship to the other digits.

COBOL (COmmon Business Oriented Language) A high level programming language for business applications.

CODASYL Refers to an international committee of people that coordinated the development of COBOL and defined an accompanying database standard.

COM Computer Output to Microform or to Microfilm.

Communication controller Title of both a person responsible for the communications facilities and service at a computer installation and a device connecting a number of data transmission lines to a computer.

Communications protocol A set of rules governing the format and sequence of messages in a data transmission system.

Compiler A program taking high level language statements of a complete program and producing machine code.

Computer A machine accepting input, automatically processing it under the control of a stored program and providing the results.

Console A terminal from which an operator controls a computer.

Control program A program which controls the operation of other programs.

Control A circuit in the central processor holding the address in memory of the next instruction to be obeyed.

Control unit Equipment controlling other devices, e.g., disk control unit. Particularly used for the controlling part of a central processor.

CORAL A programming language for military applications.

Core memory Immediate access memory using a magnetic ring for each bit stored.

Critical Path Analysis Similar to *PERT* (see PERT)

Cybernetics The mathematical science of the transmission and transformation of measurable information.

Cylinder The set of tracks, one on each magnetic surface of a disk pack, which can be accessed from one position of the recording heads.

Data Information, held or moved in a coded and structured way, representing numbers, letters and symbols.

Data capture Data collection performed in the course of a transaction.

Data collection Any form of transfer of unprocessed data into a computer system.

Data controller The person responsible in a data processing department for ensuring that all data items submitted to a computer system are correctly included in processing.

Data description language A language used in defining items in a database.

Data dictionary A list of names, definitions and characteristics of items in a database.

Data preparation Transcription by a person of information to machine readable data.

Data processing The operation of collecting data, processing it and supplying results; it is particularly used for computer processing of business information.
Data transmission Use of a communications line to send data between a computer and another computer or a terminal.
Database A collection of data structured in a way suiting the relationships between elements and the organization of the concern, independent of particular applications programs.
Database administrator A person responsible for the structure, content, integrity and security of a database.
DBMS (**D**ata**B**ase **M**anagement **S**ystem) Programs for forming, accessing and maintaining a database.
Decision table A way of representing a solution to a problem by forming a table showing the relationships between conditions and the resultant actions.
Diagnostics Facilities in software designed to aid detection of errors in programs or faults in hardware.
Digital Data that are held and manipulated as one of a set of discrete states, as in a digital computer (cf *Analog*).
Direct access External storage in which the time for retrieval of data varies little with the position of data on the device.
Direct file organization One in which the record key is the address of the record.
Disk A device storing data magnetically on concentric tracks on the surfaces of rotating circular plates.
Disk pack The exchangeable medium from a disk drive: a set of plates on a common spindle.
Documentation The formal descriptions of the requirements and design of systems and programs provided to aid development, operation and maintenance.
EBCDIC A standard 8-bit code for character representation.
Electronic mail Facility for sending the text of a document by data transmission, rather than being delivered in printed form.
Emulation Technique allowing one computer to run programs written for another of different design.
Executive Another word for control program.
Field A group of related characters treated as a unit.
File A group of related records treated as a unit.
File librarian Either a person managing a collection of magnetic tapes and disk packs, or a program keeping a list of files and their locations.
File management Programs, usually in an operating system, providing routines through which an application program can access files, and maintaining a security system for files.
Floating point Numbers held and manipulated in two parts–mantissa and exponent–allowing a greater range of magnitude and precision.
Floppy disk A magnetic storage device in which the disk itself is flexible plastic. It is a cheaper method but slower and with less capacity than disks of rigid metal, now called hard disks in contrast.
Flowchart A diagram using flowlines and standard symbols

to show the processing to be performed in a system or program.

FORTRAN A scientific high level programming language.

Gate (logic) An electronic circuit element with one output, the signal from which depends on the state of one or more inputs in accordance with the logic of the particular type of gate. Examples are AND, NAND, OR, and NOR.

Grandfather (with *father* and *son*) Updates of files, created in the last three runs of a batch processing application, which are retained for security.

Graphics terminal One that can handle pictures as well as characters.

Hard disk Contrasted to floppy disk (*see* Floppy Disk).

Hardware Computer equipment, in contrast with *software*.

Hash total A control total accumulating the same field in a group of records. The total itself is meaningless, such as a total of account numbers. Used to check data accuracy.

Head Recording head on a magnetic storage device.

Heuristic Problem solving in which the solution is found using a procedure based on a rule-of-thumb.

Hexadecimal Numbers to base 16, numbers 0 to 9 and letters A to F representing the 16 combinations of 4 bits.

Hierarchical A database with a defined relationship between records at different levels of a structure.

High level language A programming language in which statements are written in terms appropriate to the problem, and translated by a compiler or interpreter into instructions which can be directly obeyed by the computer.

Hybrid computer One capable of processing both analog and digital data.

Indexed sequential A method of organization of data on direct access external storage device.

Information The meaning to man of data.

Input Data transfer from outside the computer system, via a peripheral, to the central processor.

Instruction A coded command in a program telling the computer what data to manipulate and what operation to perform on the data.

Instruction set The range of instructions available in a particular computer.

Interpreter A program that converts individual statements of an interactive language to machine code, directly executing one statement at a time.

Interrupt A signal to the central processor causing the program currently running to wait while the interrupt is handled.

ISO7 **I**nternational **S**tandards **O**rganization **7**-bit code.

Job control language A language used to instruct the operating system on the actions to take in running a program.

Jump A departure from the normal sequence of processing the instructions in a program. The jump may either be unconditional or conditional based on the result of a test.

Key The field identifying a record.

Kimball tag A turn-around document in the form of a miniature punched card, particularly used in garment retailing.

Label A name, given by a programmer, which identifies a program statement. Used to designate the destination of a program jump instruction.
Laser checkout A supermarket cash register to which is attached an optical device incorporating a laser for reading bar marks on goods.
Leaf Lowest element in a hierarchical database structure.
Library Either the set of software available to run on a computer, or the collection of magnetic tapes and disks of data and the room in which they are kept.
Library package A program which is available to any user as part of the software of a computer.
Linear programming A technique for finding the optimum solution to a type of problem in which constraints form straight lines if plotted on a graph.
Local Area Network A group of computers linked via communication lines which have the comprehensive communication and information-sharing capabilities.
Log A security file of messages, written as each is received.
Loop A sequence of instructions which are performed repeatedly until a pre-set condition is reached.
Low level language A programming language in which statements correspond to the machine instructions built into the computer.
Machine code A program held in binary representation which can be directly recognized and obeyed by the central processor.
Magnetic ink character recognition A method of input of data by reading stylized characters printed in magnetic ink on documents, used particularly in banking.
Magnetic tape External storage device in which data are recorded serially on a strip of plastic, coated with magnetic oxide, and reeled on spools which can be removed from the tape drive.
Master file A file with fixed information and balances, input and updated in each run of a set of application programs.
Media Material onto which data are recorded for use in computer peripherals, e.g., punched cards, magnetic tape.
Memory Memory locations in the computer used for storage of data and instructions.
Merge To combine several sorted files into one, so that the result is in order without further sorting.
MICR *see* **M**agnetic **I**nk **C**haracter **R**ecognition.
Microcode A technique in which program routines in the central processor make available a complex instruction set by using sequences of operations in a simpler instruction set.
Microcomputer A computer in which the central processor, except for the memory, is all on one integrated circuit.
Modem (**MO**dulator **DEM**odulator) A device converting digital computer signals to analog for transmission on telephone lines.
Monitor *see* Control program.
Multi-access An operating system facility allowing a number of users at terminals to simultaneously run their own programs.
Multidrop To connect terminals at several locations to one

telephone line linking them all to one computer.

Multiprogramming A method allowing several programs to run apparently at the same time in a computer, the control program allowing one to proceed while another waits, e.g., for a peripheral transfer.

Node An element in a hierarchical database.

Normalization In a *relational database,* the process of reducing data structures so that no information about an item is destroyed if its position in a table is changed. In *floating point numbers,* normalization means the reduction of a mantissa to a standard form, e.g., a number over 0.1 and up to 1.

Object code *see* Machine code.

OCR *see* **O**ptical **C**haracter **R**ecognition.

Octal Number system to the base 8, representing digits 0 to 7 in 3 bits.

Off-line *see* On-line.

OMR *see* **O**ptical **M**ark **R**ecognition.

On-line In direct communication with the central processor of a computer.

Operand An item operated on by an instruction.

Operating system Programs controlling the operation of the computer system, particularly the management of files and the sequence of running the programs.

Operation code The code in an instruction specifying the operation to be performed by the central processor.

Optical Character Recognition (OCR) Input of data by reading printed characters from documents.

Optical Mark Recognition (OMR) Input of data by reading marks made by hand or machine on documents.

Output To move to a device the results of processing in a form that can be removed or used.

Overflow This occurs when an arithmetic operation is such that the result exceeds the capacity of the allocated storage.

Overlay A technique controlled by the programmer for minimizing the use of random access memory by keeping rarely used program sections on disk until needed.

Packet switched network A data transmission system in which each message carries with it the address of its destination.

Paging A technique for extending the apparent size of random access memory. Programs are broken into pages, and the operating system determines which are brought into memory.

Paper tape Tape punched with holes used for data input or output.

Parallel Applied to data transfer, it means that several bits are moved as pulses on signal lines simultaneously, e.g., a byte on 8 lines. Compare *serial* transfer, where a byte would take 8 pulses on one line.

Parameter A value of a variable affecting the operation of a program or routine which can be set before the program or routine starts.

Parity A way of checking that data have been moved or stored correctly. For *odd* parity, an extra bit is added to the byte or word to make the resultant total number of '1' bits odd. For *even* parity, the total is made even.

PASCAL An interactive high level programming language.
Peripheral Any input, output or storage device outside the central processor.
PERT (**P**roject **E**valuation and **R**eview **T**echnique) A system for planning and progressing time, resource and the cost of projects by linking activities to those which have to precede them.
PL/1 (**P**rogramming **L**anguage/**1**) A high level language for use in both commercial and scientific work.
Port *see* Channel.
Program A structured set of computer instructions providing a solution to a problem.
RAM (**R**andom **A**ccess **M**emory) A form of immediate access storage such that the program can write data to any location, and subsequently read it.
Random access In general, synonymous with *direct access,* q.v. As a file organization, it has the particular meaning of denoting one where the storage address is generated from the record key by an algorithm.
Read To obtain data from storage, or a peripheral, and leave it in the central processor.
Read Only Memory (ROM) Immediate access memory from which data can be read, but cannot be written. The data are retained when the computer is switched off.
Real time Information processing in which responses are provided immediately in reaction to input.
Record A related group of items of data held and moved as one unit.
Register A storage circuit holding data directly accessible by the control unit or arithmetic and logic unit of a processor.
Relational database One in which relationships between data items are expressed by occurrence in tables of *normalized* data, rather than by positions in hierarchical structures.
Report Program Generator (RPG) A type of commercial programming language providing a simple way of generating printed tabulations from files.
Robot A mechanical manipulator controlled by a computer.
ROM *see* **R**ead **O**nly **M**emory.
Root The highest level element in a hierarchical tree structure database.
Rounding Approximating a number to its nearest equivalent with a set number of significant figures.
RPG *see* **R**eport **P**rogram **G**enerator.
Schema The complete logical structure of a database.
Sector On a magnetic disk, the smallest part of a track which can be individually addressed.
Sequential access File organization in which records are stored and accessed in ascending order of their keys.
Serial *see* Parallel transfer. Also a file organization in which records are placed one after the other as they arrive.
Simulation Investigation of the behavior of a system by establishing and running a model of it.
Software Any computer program.
Software house A concern whose business is the writing of programs.

Source code The program statements as written by a programmer, before conversion to machine code.
Spooling An operating system facility allowing slow peripheral input and output to be diverted to external storage, for example until a printer becomes available.
Stack A list held in memory, accessed by adding or removing data at one end only.
Statement A source language instruction in a computer program.
String A field or variable containing a series of individual characters, usually text.
Structured programming Development of programs in a modular fashion, defining tasks by progressively breaking them into smaller parts.
Subroutine A self-contained section of a program written to perform a common processing task. On completion of the subroutine, processing continues at the point in the program from which the subroutine was called.
Supervisor *see* Control Program.
Systems analyst A person whose job is to analyze the information processing requirements of business and design solutions.
Systems software Programs, independent of applications, for the control of the computer, generation of programs and manipulation of data.
Table A two-dimensional array.
Tape librarian A person who looks after a library of magnetic tapes and disk packs. (*see* File librarian).
Teletex A standard for transmission of electronic mail.
Teletype (Teletypewriter) A terminal with keyboard input and printed output, and sometimes with paper tape input and output also.
Terminal A device providing both input and output facilities, connected to a computer by a data transmission line.
Timesharing *see* Multi-access.
Trace A program testing facility allowing the programmer to follow the course taken through the program as it runs.
Tree structure Hierarchical database structure in which a lower level element (child) can only be related to one upper level element (parent).
Truth table A table giving the result of a logical operation for all possible combinations of inputs.
Two's complement A way of holding negative and positive binary numbers to facilitate their addition and subtraction.
Turn-around A method of data collection in which documents sent out from a computer system include machine readable data to identify the document on return.
Utility A program performing a data manipulation, such as a file copy or sort, which is useful in a variety of applications.
Validate To check input data by comparison with the allowable or expected range of values.
Verification A method of checking data preparation by comparison of two versions of the same data entered by different operators.
Virtual storage Apparent extension of memory available

to the programmer through the use of fast disk storage.
Visual display unit A terminal with input from a keyboard and output as characters on the screen of a cathode ray tube.
Wand Hand-held optical reading head, passed over documents or labels on goods to input data.
Word A group of bits, the number of which varies with the design of the processor, treated as a group in manipulation and storage of data.
Word-processor A system for keying the text of a document into the memory of a computer. Standard sections can be added and corrections made by addition, deletion, insertion, searching and moving of letters, words and paragraphs. Also used for formatting of printed text.
Write To put data into memory or out onto a peripheral storage device.